The Survey of Public Library Fundraising Practices

ISBN: 978-1-57440-270-4
Library of Congress Control Number: 2014930503
© 2014 Primary Research Group, Inc.

TABLE OF CONTENTS

TABLE OF CONTENTS 3
LIST OF TABLES 4
THE QUESTIONNAIRE 15
SURVEY PARTICPIANTS 19
CHARACTERISTICS OF THE SAMPLE 20
SUMMARY OF MAIN FINDINGS 25
Chapter 1 – Total Fundraising and Grants Volume 33
Chapter 2 – Friends of the Library 44
Chapter 3 – Book Sales and Sales of Other Intellectual Property 56
Chapter 4 – Annual Fund Drive 71
Chapter 5 – Memorials, Tributes, and Trusts 81
Chapter 6 – Online Fundraising 91
Chapter 7 – Development or Fundraising Staff 99
Chapter 8 – Grants 103

LIST OF TABLES

Table 1.1	Of the total amount of funds raised or received in donations by the library in 2013, what percentage came from individuals?................	33
Table 1.2	Of the total amount of funds raised or received in donations by the library in 2013, what percentage came from individuals? Broken out by the existence of a "friends of the library" group.............	33
Table 1.3	Of the total amount of funds raised or received in donations by the library in 2013, what percentage came from individuals? Broken out by total annual budget of the library, including spending for salaries and materials.	33
Table 1.4	Of the total amount of funds raised or received in donations by the library in 2013, what percentage came from individuals? Broken out by the size of the population served by the library.	34
Table 1.5	Of the total amount of funds raised or received in donations by the library in 2013, what percentage came from individuals? Broken out by the amount of money raised from all sources through fundraising, grants, and donations in 2013..................................	34
Table 2.1	Of the total amount of funds raised or received in donations by the library in 2013, what percentage came from corporate grants/donations?..	35
Table 2.2	Of the total amount of funds raised or received in donations by the library in 2013, what percentage came from corporate grants/donations? Broken out by the existence of a "friends of the library" group...	35
Table 2.3	Of the total amount of funds raised or received in donations by the library in 2013, what percentage came from corporate grants/donations? Broken out by total annual budget of the library, including spending for salaries and materials.	35
Table 2.4	Of the total amount of funds raised or received in donations by the library in 2013, what percentage came from corporate grants/donations? Broken out by the size of the population served by the library..	36
Table 2.5	Of the total amount of funds raised or received in donations by the library in 2013, what percentage came from corporate grants/donations? Broken out by the amount of money raised from all sources through fundraising, grants, and donations in 2013...	36
Table 3.1	Of the total amount of funds raised or received in donations by the library in 2013, what percentage came from foundation grants?...	37
Table 3.2	Of the total amount of funds raised or received in donations by the library in 2013, what percentage came from foundation grants? Broken out by the existence of a "friends of the library" group..	37

Table 3.3	Of the total amount of funds raised or received in donations by the library in 2013, what percentage came from foundation grants? Broken out by total annual budget of the library, including spending for salaries and materials.	37
Table 3.4	Of the total amount of funds raised or received in donations by the library in 2013, what percentage came from foundation grants? Broken out by the size of the population served by the library.	38
Table 3.5	Of the total amount of funds raised or received in donations by the library in 2013, what percentage came from foundations grants? Broken out by the amount of money raised from all sources through fundraising, grants, and donations in 2013.	38
Table 4.1	Of the total amount of funds raised or received in donations by the library in 2013, what percentage came from government grants?	39
Table 4.2	Of the total amount of funds raised or received in donations by the library in 2013, what percentage came from government grants? Broken out by the existence of a "friends of the library" group.	39
Table 4.3	Of the total amount of funds raised or received in donations by the library in 2013, what percentage came from government grants? Broken out by total annual budget of the library, including spending for salaries and materials.	39
Table 4.4	Of the total amount of funds raised or received in donations by the library in 2013, what percentage came from government grants? Broken out by the size of the population served by the library.	40
Table 4.5	Of the total amount of funds raised or received in donations by the library in 2013, what percentage came from government grants? Broken out by the amount of money raised from all sources through fundraising, grants, and donations in 2013.	40
Table 5.1	If the library does have a "friends of the library" group, how many members does this organization have?	44
Table 5.2	If the library does have a "friends of the library" group, how many members does this organization have? Broken out by the existence of a "friends of the library" group.	44
Table 5.3	If the library does have a "friends of the library" group, how many members does this organization have? Broken out by total annual budget of the library, including spending for salaries and materials.	44
Table 5.4	If the library does have a "friends of the library" group, how many members does this organization have? Broken out by the size of the population served by the library.	45
Table 5.5	If the library does have a "friends of the library" group, how many members does this organization have? Broken out by the	

	amount of money raised from all sources through fundraising, grants, and donations in 2013.	45
Table 6.1	How many members have joined this group in the past year?	46
Table 6.2	How many members have joined this group in the past year? Broken out by the existence of a "friends of the library" group.	46
Table 6.3	How many members have joined this group in the past year? Broken out by total annual budget of the library, including spending for salaries and materials.	46
Table 6.4	How many members have joined this group in the past year? Broken out by the size of the population served by the library.	47
Table 6.5	How many members have joined this group in the past year? Broken out by the amount of money raised from all sources through fundraising, grants, and donations in 2013.	47
Table 7.1	How much did the friends of the library group raise for the library in 2012?	48
Table 7.2	How much did the friends of the library group raise for the library in 2012? Broken out by the existence of a "friends of the library" group.	48
Table 7.3	How much did the friends of the library group raise for the library in 2012? Broken out by total annual budget of the library, including spending for salaries and materials.	48
Table 7.4	How much did the friends of the library group raise for the library in 2012? Broken out by the size of the population served by the library.	49
Table 7.5	How much did the friends of the library group raise for the library in 2012? Broken out by the amount of money raised from all sources through fundraising, grants, and donations in 2013.	49
Table 8.1	How much did the friends of the library group raise for the library in 2013?	50
Table 8.2	How much did the friends of the library group raise for the library in 2013? Broken out by the existence of a "friends of the library" group.	50
Table 8.3	How much did the friends of the library group raise for the library in 2013? Broken out by total annual budget of the library, including spending for salaries and materials.	50
Table 8.4	How much did the friends of the library group raise for the library in 2013? Broken out by the size of the population served by the library.	51
Table 8.5	How much did the friends of the library group raise for the library in 2013? Broken out by the amount of money raised from all sources through fundraising, grants, and donations in 2013.	51
Table 9.1	How much did the library raise through book sales and the sales of other library materials such as DVDs, CDs, and magazines in 2012?	56

Table 9.2	How much did the library raise through book sales and the sales of other library materials such as DVDs, CDs, and magazines in 2012? Broken out by the existence of a "friends of the library" group.	56
Table 9.3	How much did the library raise through book sales and the sales of other library materials such as DVDs, CDs, and magazines in 2012? Broken out by total annual budget of the library, including spending for salaries and materials.	57
Table 9.4	How much did the library raise through book sales and the sales of other library materials such as DVDs, CDs, and magazines in 2012? Broken out by the size of the population served by the library.	57
Table 9.5	How much did the library raise through book sales and the sales of other library materials such as DVDs, CDs, and magazines in 2012? Broken out by the amount of money raised from all sources through fundraising, grants, and donations in 2013.	58
Table 10.1	How much did the library raise through book sales and the sales of other library materials such as DVDs, CDs, and magazines in 2013?	59
Table 10.2	How much did the library raise through book sales and the sales of other library materials such as DVDs, CDs, and magazines in 2013? Broken out by the existence of a "friends of the library" group.	59
Table 10.3	How much did the library raise through book sales and the sales of other library materials such as DVDs, CDs, and magazines in 2013? Broken out by total annual budget of the library, including spending for salaries and materials.	59
Table 10.4	How much did the library raise through book sales and the sales of other library materials such as DVDs, CDs, and magazines in 2013? Broken out by the size of the population served by the library.	60
Table 10.5	How much did the library raise through book sales and the sales of other library materials such as DVDs, CDs, and magazines in 2013? Broken out by the amount of money raised from all sources through fundraising, grants, and donations in 2013.	60
Table 11.1	Of the amount raised, approximately what percentage was from book sales?	61
Table 11.2	Of the amount raised, approximately what percentage was from book sales? Broken out by the existence of a "friends of the library" group.	61
Table 11.3	Of the amount raised, approximately what percentage was from book sales? Broken out by total annual budget of the library, including spending for salaries and materials.	61

Table 11.4	Of the amount raised, approximately what percentage was from book sales? Broken out by the size of the population served by the library.	62
Table 11.5	Of the amount raised, approximately what percentage was from book sales? Broken out by the amount of money raised from all sources through fundraising, grants, and donations in 2013.	62
Table 12.1	Of the amount raised, approximately what percentage was from periodicals?	63
Table 12.2	Of the amount raised, approximately what percentage was from periodicals? Broken out by the existence of a "friends of the library" group.	63
Table 12.3	Of the amount raised, approximately what percentage was from periodicals? Broken out by total annual budget of the library, including spending for salaries and materials.	63
Table 12.4	Of the amount raised, approximately what percentage was from periodicals? Broken out by the size of the population served by the library.	64
Table 12.5	Of the amount raised, approximately what percentage was from periodicals? Broken out by the amount of money raised from all sources through fundraising, grants, and donations in 2013.	64
Table 13.1	Of the amount raised, approximately what percentage was from sales of DVDs, CDs, and other non-print materials?	65
Table 13.2	Of the amount raised, approximately what percentage was from sales of DVDs, CDs, and other non-print materials? Broken out by the existence of a "friends of the library" group.	65
Table 13.3	Of the amount raised, approximately what percentage was from sales of DVDs, CDs, and other non-print materials? Broken out by total annual budget of the library, including spending for salaries and materials.	65
Table 13.4	Of the amount raised, approximately what percentage was from sales of DVDs, CDs, and other non-print materials? Broken out by the size of the population served by the library.	66
Table 13.5	Of the amount raised, approximately what percentage was from sales of DVDs, CDs, and other non-print materials? Broken out by the amount of money raised from all sources through fundraising, grants, and donations in 2013.	66
Table 14.1	Does the library have a book "wish list" that library patrons or browsers of the library website can view and then buy the book for the library from Amazon or some other bookseller?	67
Table 14.2	Does the library have a book "wish list" that library patrons or browsers of the library website can view and then buy the book for the library from Amazon or some other bookseller? Broken out by the existence of a "friends of the library" group.	67

The Survey of Public Library Fundraising Practices

Table 14.3	Does the library have a book "wish list" that library patrons or browsers of the library website can view and then buy the book for the library from Amazon or some other bookseller? Broken out by total annual budget of the library, including spending for salaries and materials.	67
Table 14.4	Does the library have a book "wish list" that library patrons or browsers of the library website can view and then buy the book for the library from Amazon or some other bookseller? Broken out by the size of the population served by the library.	68
Table 14.5	Does the library have a book "wish list" that library patrons or browsers of the library website can view and then buy the book for the library from Amazon or some other bookseller? Broken out by the amount of money raised from all sources through fundraising, grants, and donations in 2013	68
Table 15.1	If your library has such a wish list, how many books were purchased for the library through this system in the past year?	69
Table 15.2	If your library has such a wish list, how many books were purchased for the library through this system in the past year? Broken out by the existence of a "friends of the library" group.	69
Table 15.3	If your library has such a wish list, how many books were purchased for the library through this system in the past year? Broken out by total annual budget of the library, including spending for salaries and materials.	69
Table 15.4	If your library has such a wish list, how many books were purchased for the library through this system in the past year? Broken out by the size of the population served by the library.	70
Table 15.5	If your library has such a wish list, how many books were purchased for the library through this system in the past year? Broken out by the amount of money raised from all sources through fundraising, grants, and donations in 2013	70
Table 16.1	Does your library have an annual fund drive?	71
Table 16.2	Does your library have an annual fund drive? Broken out by the existence of a "friends of the library" group.	71
Table 16.3	Does your library have an annual fund drive? Broken out by total annual budget of the library, including spending for salaries and materials.	71
Table 16.4	Does your library have an annual fund drive? Broken out by the size of the population served by the library.	71
Table 16.5	Does your library have an annual fund drive? Broken out by the amount of money raised from all sources through fundraising, grants, and donations in 2013	72
Table 17.1	What is the budget for the annual fund drive for labor, promotion (such as direct mail), phone calls, events, entertainment, and any other costs?	73
Table 17.2	What is the budget for the annual fund drive for labor, promotion (such as direct mail), phone calls, events,	

	entertainment, and any other costs? Broken out by the existence of a "friends of the library" group.	73
Table 17.3	What is the budget for the annual fund drive for labor, promotion (such as direct mail), phone calls, events, entertainment, and any other costs? Broken out by total annual budget of the library, including spending for salaries and materials.	73
Table 17.4	What is the budget for the annual fund drive for labor, promotion (such as direct mail), phone calls, events, entertainment, and any other costs? Broken out by the size of the population served by the library.	74
Table 17.5	What is the budget for the annual fund drive for labor, promotion (such as direct mail), phone calls, events, entertainment, and any other costs? Broken out by the amount of money raised from all sources through fundraising, grants, and donations in 2013.	74
Table 18.1	How much did the library raise through the annual fund drive in 2012?	75
Table 18.2	How much did the library raise through the annual fund drive in 2012? Broken out by the existence of a "friends of the library" group.	75
Table 18.3	How much did the library raise through the annual fund drive in 2012? Broken out by total annual budget of the library, including spending for salaries and materials.	75
Table 18.4	How much did the library raise through the annual fund drive in 2012? Broken out by the size of the population served by the library.	76
Table 18.5	How much did the library raise through the annual fund drive in 2012? Broken out by the amount of money raised from all sources through fundraising, grants, and donations in 2013.	76
Table 19.1	How much did the library raise through the annual fund drive in 2013?	77
Table 19.2	How much did the library raise through the annual fund drive in 2013? Broken out by the existence of a "friends of the library" group.	77
Table 19.3	How much did the library raise through the annual fund drive in 2013? Broken out by total annual budget of the library, including spending for salaries and materials.	77
Table 19.4	How much did the library raise through the annual fund drive in 2013? Broken out by the size of the population served by the library.	78
Table 19.5	How much did the library raise through the annual fund drive in 2013? Broken out by the amount of money raised from all sources through fundraising, grants, and donations in 2013.	78
Table 20.1	How much has the library cumulatively received through naming rights over the past three years?	81

Table 20.2	How much has the library cumulatively received through naming rights over the past three years? Broken out by the existence of a "friends of the library" group.	81
Table 20.3	How much has the library cumulatively received through naming rights over the past three years? Broken out by total annual budget of the library, including spending for salaries and materials.	81
Table 20.4	How much has the library cumulatively received through naming rights over the past three years? Broken out by the size of the population served by the library.	82
Table 20.5	How much has the library cumulatively received through naming rights over the past three years? Broken out by the amount of money raised from all sources through fundraising, grants, and donations in 2013.	82
Table 21.1	How much has the library cumulatively received through memorials over the past three years?	83
Table 21.2	How much has the library cumulatively received through memorials over the past three years? Broken out by the existence of a "friends of the library" group.	83
Table 21.3	How much has the library cumulatively received through memorials over the past three years? Broken out by total annual budget of the library, including spending for salaries and materials.	83
Table 21.4	How much has the library cumulatively received through memorials over the past three years? Broken out by the size of the population served by the library.	84
Table 21.5	How much has the library cumulatively received through memorials over the past three years? Broken out by the amount of money raised from all sources through fundraising, grants, and donations in 2013.	84
Table 22.1	How much has the library cumulatively received through tributes over the past three years?	85
Table 22.2	How much has the library cumulatively received through tributes over the past three years? Broken out by the existence of a "friends of the library" group.	85
Table 22.3	How much has the library cumulatively received through tributes over the past three years? Broken out by total annual budget of the library, including spending for salaries and materials.	85
Table 22.4	How much has the library cumulatively received through tributes over the past three years? Broken out by the size of the population served by the library.	86
Table 22.5	How much has the library cumulatively received through tributes over the past three years? Broken out by the amount of money raised from all sources through fundraising, grants, and donations in 2013.	86

Table 23.1	Has any sum of money or other tangible assets been left to the library in a will or through a trust in the past five years?	87
Table 23.2	Has any sum of money or other tangible assets been left to the library in a will or through a trust in the past five years? Broken out by the existence of a "friends of the library" group.	87
Table 23.3	Has any sum of money or other tangible assets been left to the library in a will or through a trust in the past five years? Broken out by total annual budget of the library, including spending for salaries and materials.	87
Table 23.4	Has any sum of money or other tangible assets been left to the library in a will or through a trust in the past five years? Broken out by the size of the population served by the library.	88
Table 23.5	Has any sum of money or other tangible assets been left to the library in a will or through a trust in the past five years? Broken out by the amount of money raised from all sources through fundraising, grants, and donations in 2013.	88
Table 24.1	What is the monetary value of the total of what has been left to the library in wills or other bequests over the past five years?	89
Table 24.2	What is the monetary value of the total of what has been left to the library in wills or other bequests over the past five years? Broken out by the existence of a "friends of the library" group.	89
Table 24.3	What is the monetary value of the total of what has been left to the library in wills or other bequests over the past five years? Broken out by total annual budget of the library, including spending for salaries and materials.	89
Table 24.4	What is the monetary value of the total of what has been left to the library in wills or other bequests over the past five years? Broken out by the size of the population served by the library.	90
Table 24.5	What is the monetary value of the total of what has been left to the library in wills or other bequests over the past five years? Broken out by the amount of money raised from all sources through fundraising, grants, and donations in 2013.	90
Table 25.1	Does your library have a "donate" button (or similar function) on the library's website?	91
Table 25.2	Does your library have a "donate" button (or similar function) on the library's website? Broken out by the existence of a "friends of the library" group.	91
Table 25.3	Does your library have a "donate" button (or similar function) on the library's website? Broken out by total annual budget of the library, including spending for salaries and materials.	91
Table 25.4	Does your library have a "donate" button (or similar function) on the library's website? Broken out by the size of the population served by the library.	91
Table 25.5	Does your library have a "donate" button (or similar function) on the library's website? Broken out by the amount of money	

	raised from all sources through fundraising, grants, and donations in 2013. 92
Table 26.1	Does your library have a "donate" button (or similar function) on the library's Facebook page? 93
Table 27.1	Does your library have a "donate" button (or similar function) on the library's blog? 93
Table 28.1	Does your library have a "donate" button (or similar function) on the library's YouTube channel? 93
Table 29.1	How much did the library raise specifically through online donations in 2012? 94
Table 29.2	How much did the library raise specifically through online donations in 2012? Broken out by the existence of a "friends of the library" group. 94
Table 29.3	How much did the library raise specifically through online donations in 2012? Broken out by total annual budget of the library, including spending for salaries and materials. 94
Table 29.4	How much did the library raise specifically through online donations in 2012? Broken out by the size of the population served by the library. 95
Table 29.5	How much did the library raise specifically through online donations in 2012? Broken out by the amount of money raised from all sources through fundraising, grants, and donations in 2013. 95
Table 30.1	How much did the library raise specifically through online donations in 2013? 96
Table 30.2	How much did the library raise specifically through online donations in 2013? Broken out by the existence of a "friends of the library" group. 96
Table 30.3	How much did the library raise specifically through online donations in 2013? Broken out by total annual budget of the library, including spending for salaries and materials. 96
Table 30.4	How much did the library raise specifically through online donations in 2013? Broken out by the size of the population served by the library. 97
Table 30.5	How much did the library raise specifically through online donations in 2013? Broken out by the amount of money raised from all sources through fundraising, grants, and donations in 2013. 97
Table 31.1	Does the library have a fundraising or development staff? 99
Table 31.2	Does the library have a fundraising or development staff? Broken out by the existence of a "friends of the library" group. 99
Table 31.3	Does the library have a fundraising or development staff? Broken out by total annual budget of the library, including spending for salaries and materials. 99
Table 31.4	Does the library have a fundraising or development staff? Broken out by the size of the population served by the library. 99

Table 31.5	Does the library have a fundraising or development staff? Broken out by the amount of money raised from all sources through fundraising, grants, and donations in 2013	100
Table 32.1	How much did the library raise through grants in 2012?	103
Table 32.2	How much did the library raise through grants in 2012? Broken out by the existence of a "friends of the library" group.	103
Table 32.3	How much did the library raise through grants in 2012? Broken out by total annual budget of the library, including spending for salaries and materials.	103
Table 32.4	How much did the library raise through grants in 2012? Broken out by the size of the population served by the library.	104
Table 32.5	How much did the library raise through grants in 2012? Broken out by the amount of money raised from all sources through fundraising, grants, and donations in 2013	104
Table 33.1	How much did the library raise through grants in 2013?	105
Table 33.2	How much did the library raise through grants in 2013? Broken out by the existence of a "friends of the library" group.	105
Table 33.3	How much did the library raise through grants in 2013? Broken out by total annual budget of the library, including spending for salaries and materials.	105
Table 33.4	How much did the library raise through grants in 2013? Broken out by the size of the population served by the library.	106
Table 33.5	How much did the library raise through grants in 2013? Broken out by the amount of money raised from all sources through fundraising, grants, and donations in 2013	106
Table 34.1	How much manpower did the library expend in trying to obtain grants in the past year?	107
Table 34.2	How much manpower did the library expend in trying to obtain grants in the past year? Broken out by the existence of a "friends of the library" group.	107
Table 34.3	How much manpower did the library expend in trying to obtain grants in the past year? Broken out by total annual budget of the library, including spending for salaries and materials.	107
Table 34.4	How much manpower did the library expend in trying to obtain grants in the past year? Broken out by the size of the population served by the library.	108
Table 34.5	How much manpower did the library expend in trying to obtain grants in the past year? Broken out by the amount of money raised from all sources through fundraising, grants, and donations in 2013.	108

THE QUESTIONNAIRE

CHAPTER 1 – TOTAL FUNDRAISING AND GRANTS VOLUME

1. Of the total amount of funds raised or received in donations by the library in 2013, what percentage came from _____?

    A. Individuals
    B. Corporate grants/donations
    C. Foundation grants
    D. Government grants

2. Describe how the source of fundraising and donation revenue for the library has changed over the past three years.

CHAPTER 2 – FRIENDS OF THE LIBRARY

3. If the library does have a "friends of the library" group, how many members does this organization have?

4. How many members have joined this group in the past year?

5. How much did the friends of the library group raise for the library in _____?

    A. 2012
    B. 2013

6. About how often does this group meet?

7. Describe a few of your friends of the library group's most effective fundraising events.

CHAPTER 3 – BOOK SALES AND SALES OF OTHER INTELLECTUAL PROPERTY

8. How much did the library raise through book sales and the sales of other library materials such as DVDs, CDs, and magazines in _____?

    A. 2012
    B. 2013

9. Of the amount raised, approximately what percentage was from _____?

    A. Book sales

B. Periodicals
C. Sales of DVDs, CDs, and other non-print materials

10. Does the library have a book "wish list" that library patrons or browsers of the library website can view and then buy the book for the library from Amazon or some other bookseller?

11. If your library has such a wish list, how many books were purchased for the library through this system in the past year?

CHAPTER 4 – ANNUAL FUND DRIVE

12. Does your library have an annual fund drive?

13. What is the budget for the annual fund drive for labor, promotion (such as direct mail), phone calls, events, entertainment, and any other costs?

14. How much did the library raise through the annual fund drive in _____?

    A. 2012
    B. 2013

15. How has the library's annual fund strategy changed over the past five years? Is it relying more or less on direct mail? Have events come to play a more major role or not? Have costs increased or not? Comment on recent changes.

16. What is the single idea that most improved your results for your annual fund drive?

CHAPTER 5 – MEMORIALS, TRIBUTRES, AND TRUSTS

17. How much has the library cumulatively received through _____ over the past three years?

    A. Naming rights
    B. Memorials
    C. Tributes

18. Has any sum of money or other tangible assets been left to the library in a will or through a trust in the past five years?

19. What is the monetary value of the total of what has been left to the library in wills or other bequests over the past five years?

CHAPTER 6 – ONLINE FUNDRAISING

20. Does your library have a "donate" button (or similar function) on the library's _____?

    A. Website
    B. Facebook page
    C. Blog
    D. YouTube channel

21. Does your library have a "donate" button (or similar function) on any other venue?

22. How much did the library raise specifically through online donations in _____?

    A. 2012
    B. 2013

23. What has been your library's most effective means of online fundraising and how did you use it?

CHAPTER 7 – DEVELOPMENT OR FUNDRAISING STAFF

24. Does the library have a fundraising or development staff?

25. What has been the budget trend for the library's development or fundraising staff over the past two years? Has its budget increased or decreased? If so, by how much? What is the outlook for the future?

26. Please describe some of the most effective fundraising special events staged or held by the library, the friends of the library, a library foundation, or any other group.

CHAPTER 8 – GRANTS

27. How much did the library raise through grants in _____?

    A. 2012
    B. 2013

28. How much manpower did the library expend in trying to obtain grants in the past year?[*]

---

[*] If one full-time employee spent all of his/her time on grant applications, this would be 1,800 hours.

The Survey of Public Library Fundraising Practices

29. Please name some of the library's most important grants received over the past five years and, if possible, the amount and source.

30. What are your favorite information sources about library fundraising? Mention blogs, listservs, conferences, and other sources that have been useful to you.

SURVEY PARTICPIANTS

Ada Community Library
Alexander Memorial Library
Arlington Public Library
Austin Public Library
Bennington Public Library
Brentwood Library
Brillon Public Library
Butler Library
Canyon Area Library
Coralville Public Library
Crowley Public Library
Deshler Public Library
Enosburg Falls Public Library
Harlingen Public Library
Haslet Public Library
Hooker County Library
Jessie F. Hallett Memorial Library
Krum Public Library
Lawler Public Library
Library District #2 of Linn County
Marigold Library System
Millersburg Community Library
Morrill Public Library
Morton-James Public Library
Muehl Public Library
New Braunfels Public Library
Olin Public Library
Perry Public Library
Pflugerville Public Library
San Marino Public Library Foundation
Sandusky Library
Shaker Heights Public Library
Shepherd Public Library
Southside Regional Library
Spillville Public Library
Swaledale Public Library
Van Meter Public Library
Van Zandt County Library
Wahoo Public Library
Will Rogers Library
Williams Public Library

CHARACTERISTICS OF THE SAMPLE
Overall sample size: 41

By Friends of Library Group
Has a "friends of library" group	30
Does not have a "friends of library" group	11

By Budget
Less than $100,000	13
$100,000 to $499,999	14
$500,000 or more	14

By Population Served
Less than 2,500	14
2,500 to 19,999	13
20,000 or more	14

By Money Raised in 2013
Less than $5,000	13
$5,000 to $14,999	10
$15,000 to $49,999	7
$50,000 or more	11

Existence of a "friends of the library" group, broken out by the total annual budget of the library, including spending for salaries and materials.

Budget	Has a "friends of library" group	Does not have a "friends of library" group
Less than $100,000	30.77%	69.23%
$100,000 to $499,999	92.86%	7.14%
$500,000 or more	92.86%	7.14%

Existence of a "friends of the library" group, broken out by the size of the population served by the library.

Population Served	Has a "friends of library" group	Does not have a "friends of library" group
Less than 2,500	42.86%	57.14%
2,500 to 19,999	84.62%	15.38%
20,000 or more	92.86%	7.14%

Existence of a "friends of the library" group, broken out by the amount of money raised from all sources through fundraising, grants, and donations in 2013.

Money Raised in 2013	Has a "friends of library" group	Does not have a "friends of library" group
Less than $5,000	61.54%	38.46%
$5,000 to $14,999	80.00%	20.00%
$15,000 to $49,999	85.71%	14.29%
$50,000 or more	72.73%	27.27%

Total annual budget of the library, including spending for salaries and materials, broken out by the existence of a "friends of the library" group.

Friends of Library Group	Less than $100,000	$100,000 to $499,999	$500,000 or more
Has a "friends of library" group	13.33%	43.33%	43.33%
Does not have a "friends of library" group	81.82%	9.09%	9.09%

Total annual budget of the library, including spending for salaries and materials, broken out by the size of the population served by the library.

Population Served	Less than $100,000	$100,000 to $499,999	$500,000 or more
Less than 2,500	78.57%	21.43%	0.00%
2,500 to 19,999	15.38%	69.23%	15.38%
20,000 or more	0.00%	14.29%	85.71%

Total annual budget of the library, including spending for salaries and materials, broken out by the amount of money raised from all sources through fundraising, grants, and donations in 2013.

Money Raised in 2013	Less than $100,000	$100,000 to $499,999	$500,000 or more
Less than $5,000	53.85%	30.77%	15.38%
$5,000 to $14,999	30.00%	60.00%	10.00%
$15,000 to $49,999	28.57%	28.57%	42.86%
$50,000 or more	9.09%	18.18%	72.73%

Size of the population served by the library, broken out by the existence of a "friends of the library" group.

Friends of Library Group	Less than 2,500	2,500 to 19,999	20,000 or more
Has a "friends of library" group	20.00%	36.67%	43.33%
Does not have a "friends of library" group	72.73%	18.18%	9.09%

Size of the population served by the library, broken out by the total annual budget of the library, including spending for salaries and materials.

Budget	Less than 2,500	2,500 to 19,999	20,000 or more
Less than $100,000	84.62%	15.38%	0.00%
$100,000 to $499,999	21.43%	64.29%	14.29%
$500,000 or more	0.00%	14.29%	85.71%

Size of the population served by the library, broken out by the amount of money raised from all sources through fundraising, grants, and donations in 2013.

Money Raised in 2013	Less than 2,500	2,500 to 19,999	20,000 or more
Less than $5,000	61.54%	30.77%	7.69%
$5,000 to $14,999	30.00%	40.00%	30.00%
$15,000 to $49,999	28.57%	28.57%	42.86%
$50,000 or more	9.09%	27.27%	63.64%

Amount of money raised from all sources through fundraising, grants, and donations in 2013, broken out by the existence of a "friends of the library" group.

Friends of Library Group	Less than $5,000	$5,000 to $14,999	$15,000 to $49,999	$50,000 or more
Has a "friends of library" group	26.67%	26.67%	20.00%	26.67%
Does not have a "friends of library" group	45.45%	18.18%	9.09%	27.27%

Amount of money raised from all sources through fundraising, grants, and donations in 2013, broken out by the total annual budget of the library, including spending for salaries and materials.

Budget	Less than $5,000	$5,000 to $14,999	$15,000 to $49,999	$50,000 or more
Less than $100,000	53.85%	23.08%	15.38%	7.69%
$100,000 to $499,999	28.57%	42.86%	14.29%	14.29%
$500,000 or more	14.29%	7.14%	21.43%	57.14%

Amount of money raised from all sources through fundraising, grants, and donations in 2013, broken out by the size of the population served by the library.

Population Served	Less than $5,000	$5,000 to $14,999	$15,000 to $49,999	$50,000 or more
Less than 2,500	57.14%	21.43%	14.29%	7.14%
2,500 to 19,999	30.77%	30.77%	15.38%	23.08%
20,000 or more	7.14%	21.43%	21.43%	50.00%

SUMMARY OF MAIN FINDINGS

CHAPTER 1 – TOTAL FUNDRAISING AND GRANTS VOLUME

Percentage of Funds Derived from Individuals

Of the total amount of funds raised or received in donations by the libraries in our sample in 2013, our survey participants estimated that a mean of 49.1 percent came from individuals. The median, however, is a good deal lower than this figure at 35 percent, and the range is from 0 to 100. This percentage is significantly higher among those libraries in the sample with a "friends of the library" than it is for those without such a group, as the mean for the former is 53.93 percent while the mean for the latter is just 36.82 percent. When broken out by the library's annual budget, those participants with the greatest budgets ($500,000 or more) saw the highest percentage of funds come from individuals, a mean of 59 percent and a median of 70 percent, while no other breakouts in this category topped a mean of 48 percent and median 30 percent. Likewise, those libraries serving the largest populations (20,000 or more) estimated a mean of 61.92 percent of funds came from individuals, while the remaining two ranges in this category had means between 42 and 43.5 percent.

Percentage of Funds Derived from Corporate Grants/Donations

According to the libraries in the sample, a mean of just 13.14 percent of the total funds raised in 2013 were accounted for by corporate grants and donations. What's more, the median here was 0 percent, as the overall mean of was greatly affected by two large responses of 83 and 95 percent, both of which were libraries with budgets under $100,000 that raised less than $5,000 in 2013 and served populations under 2,500. In fact, of the 39 respondents, just 10 libraries responded higher than 10 percent (and only 3 higher than 50 percent). While the split between those libraries with a "friends of the library" group and those without such a group was fairly even (a mean of 12.63 percent for the former, a mean of 14.45 percent for the latter), this figure drops steadily as the library budget increases: 19.23 percent for those with budgets less than $100,000, down to a mean of 13.73 percent for the middle range ($100,000 to $499,999) and down again to a mean of 6.46 percent for those libraries with budgets of $500,000 or more.

Percentage of Funds Derived from Foundation Grants

For the libraries in our sample, a healthy amount of funds are derived from foundation grants, with a mean of 29.19 percent coming from these sources. However, the median is nearly a third of this figure at just 10 percent. Those libraries without a "friends of the library" group attribute a significant amount of funds from foundation grants, a mean of 43.18 percent and a mean of 40 percent, as compared to a mean of only 23.7 percent for those libraries with such groups and a median of just 2.5 percent. While a mean between 33 and 34 percent of funds for libraries serving populations under 20,000 are derived from foundation grants, this figure drops to 20.58 percent for the top population range here (20,000 or more). As the amount of money raised in 2013 by the library increases, so too does the mean percentage that came from foundation grants, from a low of 14.27 percent for those raising less than $5,000, up to a high of 43.86 percent among those raising $15,000 to $49,999. The anomaly here is the top bracket (those libraries that raised $50,000 or more), where the mean drops to 31.64 percent.

Percentage of Funds Derived from Government Grants

A mean of just 8.54 percent of the funds raised by participating libraries in 2013 was derived from government grants, and this is taking into account one participant's response of 90 percent. In fact, 29 of the 39 respondents for this question answered 0 percent, and just 4 responded with 50 percent or higher, 3 of which raised less than $5,000 overall.

CHAPTER 2 – FRIENDS OF THE LIBRARY

Membership for the Friends of the Library Group

Among those libraries in the sample with a "friends of the library" group (of which there are 30 altogether), the mean number of members in such a group is 79.12. However, this mean is greatly offset by one participant's response of 500, and just 7 other libraries answered higher than 50. Thus, the median is less than a third of the mean here at 25. The range is from 5 to 500. Not surprisingly, the number of members in the "friends of the library" rises steadily as the library's budget increases, from a mean of 8.25 members for those with budgets under $100,000, up to 45.08 for those in the middle budget range ($100,000 to $499,999) and then more than tripling to a mean of 156 for the top budget range ($500,000 or more). This same relationship applies to the size of the population served by the library: from a mean of 14 for the bottom range (less than 2,500) up to a mean of 183.25 for the top range (20,000 or more). Broken out by the amount of money raised by the library in 2013, the mean is between 42.5 and 44.25 for those libraries that raised less than $15,000, a figure that jumps to 81.5 for the next range ($15,000 to $49,999) before more than doubling to 176 for the top range ($50,000 or more).

The libraries in the sample estimate that a mean of 17 members have joined the library's "friends of the library" group in the past year. While two participants cited as many as 100 new members during this time, and another library reported 70 new members, no other library in the sample responded with more than 20. All three of these libraries had budgets of at least $500,000, raised at least $50,000 in 2013, and serve a population of at least 20,000. So again, those libraries with the largest budgets saw the biggest increase in membership for these "friends of the library" groups, as did those libraries that raised the most money and serve the largest populations.

Money Raised by the "Friends of the Library" Group

The "friends of the library" groups raised a mean of $13,366 each for the libraries in the sample in 2013. The median here was $6,000. Both of these figures were a slight increase from 2012, where the mean was $12,359 and the median $5,000. As the library's budget increases, there is a steady increase in the amount of money raised by these groups, from a mean of $1,575 for the lowest budget range (less than $100,000) up to $4,962 for the middle range ($100,000 to $499,999) and a mean of $29,009 for the top library budget range ($500,000 or more). The same can be said when the data is broken out by the size of the population served by the library: a mean of $1,633 was raised by those groups associated with libraries serving populations under 2,500, which jumps to $8,150 for the middle range (2,500 to 19,999) and then more than triples to $26,144 for the top range (20,000 or more). These figures for 2013 were all comparable to the data for 2012.

CHAPTER 3 – BOOK SALES AND SALES OF OTHER INTELLECTUAL PROPERTY

Money Raised Through Book Sales and Other Library Materials

In 2013, the libraries in the sample raised a mean of $6,660 through the sale of books and all other library materials, including DVDs, CDs, and magazines. The median, however, was $950. Overall, 18 of 36 respondents raised less than $1,000, while 6 participants raised $10,000 or more, including two libraries that raised $60,000 and $80,000, respectively. No library without a "friends of the library" group raised more than $5,700, nor did any library serving a population under 20,000 or with an annual budget under $500,000 raise more than $8,000 in this respect. Interestingly, those libraries in the sample that raised less than $5,000 in fundraising, grants, and donations raised a mean of $5,226 from the sale of books, DVDs, CDs, and magazines, the only breakout in this category with a mean higher than the amount raised through fundraising.

Percentage of Money Raised from Book Sales

Of this total money raised, the libraries in the sample estimated that a mean of 84.25 percent was from the sale of books. The median, however, was even higher at 95 percent, as 16 of the 27 respondents answered 90 percent or higher (and 14 answered 95 percent or higher). In fact, just one participant answered that less than 50 percent of this money was raised through the sale of books. Those libraries with a "friends of the library" group had a higher mean here at 87.08 percent, compared to a mean of 76.14 percent for those libraries without such a group. There was not a great difference when the data was broken out by the library's annual budget, as all three categories had means between 82 and 86.1 percent. Those libraries in the sample that raised at least $15,000 in fundraising estimated that a mean of 90 percent of the overall money raised from the sale of library materials was attributed to book sales.

Percentage of Money Raised from Other Sources

This left very little room for the sale of other materials, as libraries estimated that a mean of just 4.83 percent of the overall amount raised from the sale of library materials was from the sale of periodicals. While one participant put this figure at 100 percent, all other participants were at 6.67 percent or lower, with 20 of them responding with either 0 or 1 percent.

A mean of 10.1 percent of this overall money raised was due to the sale of DVDs, CDs, and other non-print materials. This figure increased steadily as both the library's annual budget and the population served by the library increased. For instance, while a mean of just 6.78 percent of the money raised from the sale of library materials by participants with budgets under $100,000 was through the sale of DVDs, CDs, and non-print materials, this mean was up to 10.4 percent for the middle budget range ($100,000 to $499,999) and up again to 13.46 percent for the top budget range ($500,000 or more).

Library Wish Lists

Just 14.63 percent of participants have a book "wish list" that is made available to patrons to purchase for the library. Such a list is more common among libraries serving larger populations, as 21.43 percent of those libraries serving populations of 20,000 or more have one, compared to just 7.69 percent of those libraries serving populations of 2,500 to 19,999 people. Likewise, libraries with larger budgets are more apt to have a wish list, as 21.43 percent of those with budgets of $500,000 or more do while just 7.14 percent of those with budgets in the $100,000 to $499,999 range can say the same. Libraries without a "friends of the library" group are slightly more likely to make these lists available to patrons, with 18.18 percent of them having such lists, as compared to just 13.33 percent of those libraries with a "friends of the library" group.

Among those libraries in the sample that do have a book wish list, the mean number of books that have been purchased for the library through this system in the past year is 3,022. This mean, however, is greatly offset by one participant's response of 18,000. The other respondents reported much more modest numbers: 0, 2, 5, 58, and 68.

CHAPTER 4 – ANNUAL FUND DRIVE

Annual Fund Drive

9.76 percent of all libraries in the sample have an annual fund drive. Those libraries that do have such a drive tend to be the larger libraries, as no library with an annual budget under $100,000 has one, nor do any libraries that serve populations less than 2,500 or libraries that raise less than $5,000 through fundraising. Generally speaking, as all these metrics increase, so too does the likelihood of the library having an annual fund drive: 7.14 percent of those libraries in the $100,000 to $499,999 budget range have a fund drive, a figure which jumps to 21.43 percent for the top budget range ($500,000 or more). Broken out by population served, the figures are nearly identical: 7.69 percent for the middle range (2,500 to 19,999), 21.43 percent for the top range (20,000 or more).

These 4 libraries in the sample that do have an annual fund drive raised a mean of $14,700 in 2012. The totals were as follows: $1,500; $3,735; $12,000; and $41,566.

CHAPTER 5 – MEMORIALS, TRIBUTES, AND TRUSTS

Naming Rights

Just four libraries in the sample received any money at all over the past three years through naming rights, all four of which raised at least $5,000 from fundraising and serve populations of at least 2,500 people. 35 participants did not receive any money in this respect (one participant did not answer the question). The four totals were as follows: $1,860; $10,000; $50,000; and $500,000. This resulted in an overall sample mean of $14,407.

Memorials

Over this same time span, the libraries in the sample received a mean of $4,507 through memorials. While this mean is lower than the mean for naming rights, overall there was more activity here, as 29 of 39 respondents received any money at all and 19 received at least $1,000. The median here was $800, and the maximum was $60,000, reported by one library with a budget under $100,000 that serves a population less than 2,500 yet raised $50,000 or more in fundraising in 2013. The more money the libraries in the sample raised through fundraising in 2013, the money the libraries received through memorials over the past three years, from a mean of $1,565 for those that raised less than $5,000 up to a mean of $9,856 for those that raised $50,000 or more.

Tributes

While ten libraries in the sample received any money over the past three years through tributes, only half of those received more than $500 and the maximum was just $5,000, resulting in an overall mean of only $333. The median was $0, which remained the same for every breakout category for this question.

Trusts and Wills

Nearly half (46.34 percent) of all survey participants say that any amount of money (or other tangible assets) has been left to the library in a will or through a trust over the past five years. This figure is nearly evenly split between those libraries with a "friends of the library" group (46.67 percent) and those without such a group (45.45 percent). However, while 50 percent of all those libraries with budgets of at least $100,000 say such money has been left to them via wills or trusts, just 38.46 percent of all other participants can say the same. This split is even more drastic when the data is broken out by the size of the population served by the library: between 53.85 and 57.14 percent of those libraries servicing populations of at least 2,500 people say they have received such money, as compared to just 28.57 percent of those libraries serving populations under 2,500.

Among those libraries that have received any amount of money over the past five years through a trust or will, the mean amount received during that time was $94,908. The median was $35,000, and the range was from a minimum of $500 to a maximum of $775,000. The second highest total was $365,393. The means are once again nearly even when broken out by those libraries having a "friends of the library" group ($93,958) and those that do not ($97,379). While those libraries with an annual budget under $100,000 received a mean of just $22,600 in this regard, this mean jumps to a high of $146,000 for those libraries in the $100,000 to $499,999 budget range. A similar relationship is found when the data is broken out by the size of the population served: a mean of $15,750 for the smallest range (less than 2,500), and a mean of $151,000 for the middle range (2,500 to 19,999).

CHAPTER 6 – ONLINE FUNDRAISING

Donate Button on the Library's Website

6 of 41 survey participants (14.63 percent) say the library has a "donate" button (or similar function) on the library's website. All of these are libraries with a "friends of the library" group, have annual budgets of at least $100,000, and serve populations of at least 2,500. What's more, all six of these participants raised at least $15,000 through fundraising in 2013. Of particular note is that 35.71 percent of libraries with budgets of at least $500,000 and that serve populations of 20,000 or more have such a function on the website.

Donate Button on Other Forums

No libraries in the sample have a "donate" button on the library's Facebook page, blog, or YouTube channel. A small number reported having such a button on the "friends of the library" group's website.

Online Donations

In 2013, the libraries in the sample raised a mean of $994.44 through online donations. This average was largely the work of just four participants, each with donations of at least $1,600 (and a maximum of $8,000). Only one other participant raised anything at all, and this a modest $500. Overall, the median here was $0. Still, the mean in 2013 was a slight increase from that in 2012, when survey participants raised a mean of $808.56 through online donations (and a maximum of $5,254). For 2013, as with 2012, all the libraries that raised any money through online donations have a "friends of the library" group, and all have budgets of at least $100,000 and serve populations of 2,500 or greater.

CHAPTER 7 – DEVELOPMENT OR FUNDRAISING STAFF

Fundraising Staff

Just 4 of 41 survey participants (9.76 percent) say the library has a fundraising or development staff, all of which have a "friends of the library" group. Three of these libraries have budgets of at least $500,000, serve populations of at least 20,000 people, and raised $50,000 or more through fundraising in 2013.

CHAPTER 8 – GRANTS

Money Raised Through Grants in 2013

The libraries in the sample raised a mean of $27,775 through grants in 2013, a marginal increase from the sample mean of $27,500 in 2012. While 24 of 35 respondents raised at least $500 in 2013 (and 13 of those raised at least $5,000), the remaining 11 respondents did not raise any money at all through grants, resulting in an overall median of $1,000. Still, there were some big gainers here, with three participants raising more than $100,000, including a maximum of $383,624. Those libraries with a "friends of the library" group raised significantly more than those without, with means of $35,199 for the former group and $11,575 for the latter. On average, the libraries with the largest budgets raised the most money in this regard: those libraries with budgets under $100,000 raised a mean of just $1,981, a mean which leaped to $20,224 for the middle budget range ($100,000 to $499,999) and then more than tripled to $62,010 for the top budget range ($500,000 or more). A similar trend occurs when the data is broken out by the size of the population served by the library, as those libraries serving populations less than 2,500 raised a mean of $3,801 while those libraries serving populations of 20,000 or more raised a mean of $61,527.

Manpower Expended in Obtaining Grants

We asked our survey participants how much manpower the library expended in the past year trying to obtain grants. For reference, one full-time employee spending all of his/her time on grant applications would total 1,800 hours. The libraries in the sample spent a mean of 202 hours (and a median of 50 hours). The range was from 0 to 1,560, indicating that no libraries in the sample spent the equivalent of one full-time employee's complete efforts. While those libraries with a "friends of the library" group had a higher mean than those without such a group (242 to 123, respectively), the medians favored the latter, 55 to 40. Overall, of the 30 respondents, 17 reported totals of 50 hours or less, 9 of which were either 1 hour or no time at all. Two participants did report times of 1,390 and 1,560, however, both of which were libraries with budgets of at least $500,000 and that raised at least $50,000 or more through fundraising or grants in 2013. However, outside of these two participants, the mean number of hours spent on obtaining grants when broken out by total amount of money raised in 2013 are relatively equal: while those libraries that raised less than $5,000 expended a mean of 119 hours in this respect, those libraries that raised $5,000 to $14,999 spent an average of 103 hours here and those that raised $15,000 to $49,999 spent a mean of 108 hours.

Chapter 1 – Total Fundraising and Grants Volume

Table 1.1 Of the total amount of funds raised or received in donations by the library in 2013, what percentage came from individuals?

	Mean	Median	Minimum	Maximum
Entire sample	49.10%	35.00%	0.00%	100.00%

Table 1.2 Of the total amount of funds raised or received in donations by the library in 2013, what percentage came from individuals? Broken out by the existence of a "friends of the library" group.

Friends of Library Group	Mean	Median	Minimum	Maximum
Has a "friends of library" group	53.93	53.00	0.00	100.00
Does not have a "friends of library" group	36.82	24.00	0.00	100.00

Table 1.3 Of the total amount of funds raised or received in donations by the library in 2013, what percentage came from individuals? Broken out by total annual budget of the library, including spending for salaries and materials.

Budget	Mean	Median	Minimum	Maximum
Less than $100,000	48.00%	30.00%	0.00%	100.00%
$100,000 to $499,999	40.31%	30.00%	0.00%	100.00%
$500,000 or more	59.00%	70.00%	0.00%	100.00%

Table 1.4 Of the total amount of funds raised or received in donations by the library in 2013, what percentage came from individuals? Broken out by the size of the population served by the library.

Population Served	Mean	Median	Minimum	Maximum
Less than 2,500	43.14%	28.50%	0.00%	100.00%
2,500 to 19,999	42.17%	40.00%	0.00%	100.00%
20,000 or more	61.92%	80.00%	0.00%	100.00%

Table 1.5 Of the total amount of funds raised or received in donations by the library in 2013, what percentage came from individuals? Broken out by the amount of money raised from all sources through fundraising, grants, and donations in 2013.

Money Raised in 2013	Mean	Median	Minimum	Maximum
Less than $5,000	44.91%	30.00%	0.00%	100.00%
$5,000 to $14,999	54.70%	62.50%	0.00%	100.00%
$15,000 to $49,999	51.71%	33.00%	0.00%	100.00%
$50,000 or more	46.55%	35.00%	2.00%	100.00%

Table 2.1 Of the total amount of funds raised or received in donations by the library in 2013, what percentage came from corporate grants/donations?

	Mean	Median	Minimum	Maximum
Entire sample	13.14%	0.00%	0.00%	95.00%

Table 2.2 Of the total amount of funds raised or received in donations by the library in 2013, what percentage came from corporate grants/donations? Broken out by the existence of a "friends of the library" group.

Friends of Library Group	Mean	Median	Minimum	Maximum
Has a "friends of library" group	12.63%	0.50%	0.00%	95.00%
Does not have a "friends of library" group	14.45%	0.00%	0.00%	83.00%

Table 2.3 Of the total amount of funds raised or received in donations by the library in 2013, what percentage came from corporate grants/donations? Broken out by total annual budget of the library, including spending for salaries and materials.

Budget	Mean	Median	Minimum	Maximum
Less than $100,000	19.23%	0.00%	0.00%	95.00%
$100,000 to $499,999	13.73%	5.00%	0.00%	50.00%
$500,000 or more	6.46%	0.00%	0.00%	50.00%

Table 2.4 Of the total amount of funds raised or received in donations by the library in 2013, what percentage came from corporate grants/donations? Broken out by the size of the population served by the library.

Population Served	Mean	Median	Minimum	Maximum
Less than 2,500	19.00%	0.00%	0.00%	95.00%
2,500 to 19,999	9.75%	3.00%	0.00%	50.00%
20,000 or more	9.96%	0.00%	0.00%	50.00%

Table 2.5 Of the total amount of funds raised or received in donations by the library in 2013, what percentage came from corporate grants/donations? Broken out by the amount of money raised from all sources through fundraising, grants, and donations in 2013.

Money Raised in 2013	Mean	Median	Minimum	Maximum
Less than $5,000	23.55%	0.00%	0.00%	95.00%
$5,000 to $14,999	12.35%	0.50%	0.00%	50.00%
$15,000 to $49,999	3.14%	0.00%	0.00%	17.00%
$50,000 or more	9.82%	5.00%	0.00%	50.00%

Table 3.1 Of the total amount of funds raised or received in donations by the library in 2013, what percentage came from foundation grants?

	Mean	Median	Minimum	Maximum
Entire sample	29.19%	10.00%	0.00%	100.00%

Table 3.2 Of the total amount of funds raised or received in donations by the library in 2013, what percentage came from foundation grants? Broken out by the existence of a "friends of the library" group.

Friends of Library Group	Mean	Median	Minimum	Maximum
Has a "friends of library" group	23.70%	2.50%	0.00%	100.00%
Does not have a "friends of library" group	43.18%	40.00%	0.00%	100.00%

Table 3.3 Of the total amount of funds raised or received in donations by the library in 2013, what percentage came from foundation grants? Broken out by total annual budget of the library, including spending for salaries and materials.

Budget	Mean	Median	Minimum	Maximum
Less than $100,000	28.85%	0.00%	0.00%	100.00%
$100,000 to $499,999	38.19%	44.00%	0.00%	92.00%
$500,000 or more	20.54%	5.00%	0.00%	100.00%

Table 3.4 Of the total amount of funds raised or received in donations by the library in 2013, what percentage came from foundation grants? Broken out by the size of the population served by the library.

Population Served	Mean	Median	Minimum	Maximum
Less than 2,500	33.64%	22.50%	0.00%	100.00%
2,500 to 19,999	33.33%	22.00%	0.00%	92.00%
20,000 or more	20.58%	5.00%	0.00%	100.00%

Table 3.5 Of the total amount of funds raised or received in donations by the library in 2013, what percentage came from foundation grants? Broken out by the amount of money raised from all sources through fundraising, grants, and donations in 2013.

Money Raised in 2013	Mean	Median	Minimum	Maximum
Less than $5,000	14.27%	0.00%	0.00%	73.00%
$5,000 to $14,999	32.65%	12.50%	0.00%	100.00%
$15,000 to $49,999	43.86%	65.00%	0.00%	100.00%
$50,000 or more	31.64%	20.00%	0.00%	92.00%

Table 4.1 Of the total amount of funds raised or received in donations by the library in 2013, what percentage came from government grants?

	Mean	Median	Minimum	Maximum
Entire sample	8.54%	0.00%	0.00%	90.00%

Table 4.2 Of the total amount of funds raised or received in donations by the library in 2013, what percentage came from government grants? Broken out by the existence of a "friends of the library" group.

Friends of Library Group	Mean	Median	Minimum	Maximum
Has a "friends of library" group	9.71%	0.00%	0.00%	90.00%
Does not have a "friends of library" group	5.55%	0.00%	0.00%	50.00%

Table 4.3 Of the total amount of funds raised or received in donations by the library in 2013, what percentage came from government grants? Broken out by total annual budget of the library, including spending for salaries and materials.

Budget	Mean	Median	Minimum	Maximum
Less than $100,000	3.85%	0.00%	0.00%	50.00%
$100,000 to $499,999	7.77%	0.00%	0.00%	90.00%
$500,000 or more	14.00%	0.00%	0.00%	52.00%

Table 4.4 Of the total amount of funds raised or received in donations by the library in 2013, what percentage came from government grants? Broken out by the size of the population served by the library.

Population Served	Mean	Median	Minimum	Maximum
Less than 2,500	4.14%	0.00%	0.00%	50.00%
2,500 to 19,999	14.75%	0.00%	0.00%	90.00%
20,000 or more	7.54%	0.00%	0.00%	52.00%

Table 4.5 Of the total amount of funds raised or received in donations by the library in 2013, what percentage came from government grants? Broken out by the amount of money raised from all sources through fundraising, grants, and donations in 2013.

Money Raised in 2013	Mean	Median	Minimum	Maximum
Less than $5,000	17.27%	0.00%	0.00%	90.00%
$5,000 to $14,999	0.30%	0.00%	0.00%	3.00%
$15,000 to $49,999	1.14%	0.00%	0.00%	8.00%
$50,000 or more	12.00%	0.00%	0.00%	52.00%

Describe how the source of fundraising and donation revenue for the library has changed over the past three years.

1. The source of revenue for the past three years has been consistent with FY2013 (October 2012 - September 2013) described above.

2. Not much.

3. It hasn't changed.

4. Major oil activity in our region has resulted in many local people becoming very wealthy due to leasing their land and mineral rights. Since we are a 501(c)(3) non-profit charitable organization, we have received many monetary gifts in order for those individuals to obtain tax write-offs. When people learned of our need to upgrade our 40-year-old HVAC and lighting in the building, large donations were received for that purpose, especially in 2012.

5. There as been an increase in donation revenue each year.

6. It has not changed.

7. We have formed a Friends Foundation for the Library which is our 501 c-3 fundraising arm-this has made a HUGE difference in the services, programming, materials and technology we are able to provide to our patrons.

8. It has not changed much. We had an individual leave us money in her will in 2013.

9. Foundation grants have gone done with the interest rates.

10. The main source of our fundraising has always been individuals and families.

11. People aren't donating, harder to get grants and donations.

12. It hasn't.

13. Decreasing.

14. It is much harder to get local business donations. They have everyone in town asking for money and they have a very small amount. Corporate and Foundations also seem to have less money to donate - or they have more people asking.

15. It has changed very little. We don't intentionally fundraise ~ rely on gifts from individuals and the Friends of the Library.

16. I began my director-ship in November 2012; the former director was not comfortable with grant writing so she didn't do it often. I regularly check the library grant list to see what is available.

17. We have to rely more on individuals and corporations as we have not been successful in getting Foundation Grants and the Government no longer gives us grant money.

18. This past year, the library has been more aggressive about seeking donations and grants. We have renovated a complete area of the library, creating a larger and more inviting children's space. This project entailed new carpeting, painting, a mural, shelving, children's computers and a new entryway. It was paid for completely using grants and donations. Our Friends Group provided the funding for painting the entire library. We are now applying for more grants and working on writing and developing these grants in a more professional manner.

19. It has not changed.

20. Surprisingly it has been good, considering the economic conditions in our country.

21. We have had a couple of community donors give to our library. That has been missing in the past. Usually it's a nickel and dime kind of fundraising effort.

22. It has stayed mostly the same for us with people giving money in memory of family, etc. and each year we have received a $500 amount anonymously through the Mullen Community foundation.

23. Pretty much stayed the same.

24. We have seen a decline in grant revenue and a downward turn in contributions from the Friends of the Library (counted as Individuals above. Other donations tend to fluctuate from year to year.

25. Staff fatigue – dwindling.

26. State funding has ceased - loan star program.

27. We are a relatively new library in a small community so there has been no change in how we've done our fundraising. We get a grant from the Eastern Iowa Grant Foundation and from a breakfast fundraiser we hold.

28. No changes - donations and government filtering grants.

29. Our library has more than doubled in size over the past 3 years and as we've gotten bigger we've had fewer appropriate grant opportunities.

30. Other than the annual book sale, we do not fundraise. Our library has an endowment fund.

31. It has remained steady.

32. Fundraising is done primarily through grant writing activities. More corporate grants have been awarded in the last three years than in previous years. Although corporate grants are smaller than foundation grants, that category is growing while foundation grants are falling.

33. I find it more difficult to find grants that fit our needs and the competition has increased.

34. The great increase from 2012 to 2013 was due to receiving two bequests in 2013--a very unique occurrence. Otherwise, donations were pretty stable, mostly care of individuals giving to our Friends groups and library branches.

35. Deshler Library filled out a grant for new computers, printers, 2 desks and an ADA computer. This was from the Gates Foundation and we are told they will not be having one again like this for libraries. Our donations come from putting jars in the bank and grocery store, articles in the local paper and word of mouth. There are still grants out there that we will have to look into in the future to keep our technology and library up-to-date.

36. Steady.

Chapter 2 – Friends of the Library

Table 5.1 If the library does have a "friends of the library" group, how many members does this organization have?

	Mean	Median	Minimum	Maximum
Entire sample	79.12	25.00	5.00	500.00

Table 5.2 If the library does have a "friends of the library" group, how many members does this organization have? Broken out by the existence of a "friends of the library" group.

Friends of Library Group	Mean	Median	Minimum	Maximum
Has a "friends of library" group	79.12	25.00	5.00	500.00
Does not have a "friends of library" group	N/A	N/A	N/A	N/A

Table 5.3 If the library does have a "friends of the library" group, how many members does this organization have? Broken out by total annual budget of the library, including spending for salaries and materials.

Budget	Mean	Median	Minimum	Maximum
Less than $100,000	8.25	9.00	5.00	10.00
$100,000 to $499,999	45.08	28.50	6.00	200.00
$500,000 or more	156.00	125.00	10.00	500.00

Table 5.4 If the library does have a "friends of the library" group, how many members does this organization have? Broken out by the size of the population served by the library.

Population Served	Mean	Median	Minimum	Maximum
Less than 2,500	14.00	10.00	5.00	40.00
2,500 to 19,999	38.91	15.00	6.00	200.00
20,000 or more	183.25	162.50	23.00	500.00

Table 5.5 If the library does have a "friends of the library" group, how many members does this organization have? Broken out by the amount of money raised from all sources through fundraising, grants, and donations in 2013.

Money Raised in 2013	Mean	Median	Minimum	Maximum
Less than $5,000	44.25	11.50	6.00	250.00
$5,000 to $14,999	42.50	45.00	10.00	85.00
$15,000 to $49,999	81.50	36.50	5.00	200.00
$50,000 or more	176.00	125.00	10.00	500.00

Table 6.1 How many members have joined this group in the past year?

	Mean	Median	Minimum	Maximum
Entire sample	17.00	4.00	0.00	100.00

Table 6.2 How many members have joined this group in the past year? Broken out by the existence of a "friends of the library" group.

Friends of Library Group	Mean	Median	Minimum	Maximum
Has a "friends of library" group	17.00	4.00	0.00	100.00
Does not have a "friends of library" group	N/A	N/A	N/A	N/A

Table 6.3 How many members have joined this group in the past year? Broken out by total annual budget of the library, including spending for salaries and materials.

Budget	Mean	Median	Minimum	Maximum
Less than $100,000	2.50	2.00	0.00	6.00
$100,000 to $499,999	6.17	3.50	1.00	20.00
$500,000 or more	43.86	20.00	2.00	100.00

Table 6.4 How many members have joined this group in the past year? Broken out by the size of the population served by the library.

Population Served	Mean	Median	Minimum	Maximum
Less than 2,500	4.00	2.50	0.00	15.00
2,500 to 19,999	5.64	3.00	2.00	20.00
20,000 or more	50.83	45.00	5.00	100.00

Table 6.5 How many members have joined this group in the past year? Broken out by the amount of money raised from all sources through fundraising, grants, and donations in 2013.

Money Raised in 2013	Mean	Median	Minimum	Maximum
Less than $5,000	10.75	2.50	0.00	70.00
$5,000 to $14,999	7.17	5.50	2.00	15.00
$15,000 to $49,999	8.50	7.00	0.00	20.00
$50,000 or more	45.60	20.00	3.00	100.00

Table 7.1 How much did the friends of the library group raise for the library in 2012?

	Mean	Median	Minimum	Maximum
Entire sample	$12,359.26	$5,000.00	$500.00	$80,000.00

Table 7.2 How much did the friends of the library group raise for the library in 2012? Broken out by the existence of a "friends of the library" group.

Friends of Library Group	Mean	Median	Minimum	Maximum
Has a "friends of library" group	$12,359.26	$5,000.00	$500.00	$80,000.00
Does not have a "friends of library" group	N/A	N/A	N/A	N/A

Table 7.3 How much did the friends of the library group raise for the library in 2012? Broken out by total annual budget of the library, including spending for salaries and materials.

Budget	Mean	Median	Minimum	Maximum
Less than $100,000	$1,650.00	$550.00	$500.00	$5,000.00
$100,000 to $499,999	$4,838.46	$5,000.00	$600.00	$12,000.00
$500,000 or more	$26,420.00	$17,000.00	$2,000.00	$80,000.00

Table 7.4 How much did the friends of the library group raise for the library in 2012? Broken out by the size of the population served by the library.

Population Served	Mean	Median	Minimum	Maximum
Less than 2,500	$1,766.67	$800.00	$500.00	$5,000.00
2,500 to 19,999	$5,627.27	$5,000.00	$600.00	$19,000.00
20,000 or more	$26,120.00	$14,500.00	$4,500.00	$80,000.00

Table 7.5 How much did the friends of the library group raise for the library in 2012? Broken out by the amount of money raised from all sources through fundraising, grants, and donations in 2013.

Money Raised in 2013	Mean	Median	Minimum	Maximum
Less than $5,000	$9,925.00	$3,500.00	$500.00	$55,000.00
$5,000 to $14,999	$4,950.00	$4,750.00	$600.00	$12,000.00
$15,000 to $49,999	$7,200.00	$6,350.00	$500.00	$15,000.00
$50,000 or more	$34,300.00	$30,000.00	$2,500.00	$80,000.00

Table 8.1 How much did the friends of the library group raise for the library in 2013?

	Mean	Median	Minimum	Maximum
Entire sample	$13,366.41	$6,000.00	$0.00	$80,000.00

Table 8.2 How much did the friends of the library group raise for the library in 2013? Broken out by the existence of a "friends of the library" group.

Friends of Library Group	Mean	Median	Minimum	Maximum
Has a "friends of library" group	$13,366.41	$6,000.00	$0.00	$80,000.00
Does not have a "friends of library" group	N/A	N/A	N/A	N/A

Table 8.3 How much did the friends of the library group raise for the library in 2013? Broken out by total annual budget of the library, including spending for salaries and materials.

Budget	Mean	Median	Minimum	Maximum
Less than $100,000	$1,575.00	$450.00	$400.00	$5,000.00
$100,000 to $499,999	$4,961.54	$5,000.00	$0.00	$10,000.00
$500,000 or more	$29,009.30	$17,371.00	$2,000.00	$80,000.00

Table 8.4 How much did the friends of the library group raise for the library in 2013? Broken out by the size of the population served by the library.

Population Served	Mean	Median	Minimum	Maximum
Less than 2,500	$1,633.33	$450.00	$0.00	$5,000.00
2,500 to 19,999	$8,150.09	$5,000.00	$750.00	$42,651.00
20,000 or more	$26,144.20	$14,500.00	$4,700.00	$80,000.00

Table 8.5 How much did the friends of the library group raise for the library in 2013? Broken out by the amount of money raised from all sources through fundraising, grants, and donations in 2013.

Money Raised in 2013	Mean	Median	Minimum	Maximum
Less than $5,000	$10,318.75	$3,500.00	$400.00	$60,000.00
$5,000 to $14,999	$5,281.25	$5,500.00	$750.00	$10,000.00
$15,000 to $49,999	$7,366.67	$7,350.00	$0.00	$15,000.00
$50,000 or more	$38,378.60	$42,651.00	$3,500.00	$80,000.00

About how often does this group meet?

1. Quarterly.

2. Once a month.

3. Quarterly.

4. Rarely.

5. Whenever they are planning a project, such as selling popcorn and candy at Krum Movie Nights.

6. Usually once per month.

7. Generally monthly.

8. 5 times per year.

9. Quarterly.

10. Monthly.

11. 4 times a year.

12. 1 x month.

13. Monthly.

14. About 8 times a year usually.

15. Monthly.

16. Monthly.

17. The Board meets monthly; the entire membership is invited to the annual meeting.

18. Once every other month.

19. At least twice a year and sometimes more when the need arises.

20. Every two months.

21. Once a month.

22. Monthly.

23. Our system has six locations, four of which have Friends groups. I believe they meet as follows: 1) every month except June, July, August; 2) every other month except November and December; 3) every month except June, July, August; 4) only once per year.

24. Monthly, September through May.

25. Monthly.

26. Quarterly.

27. 3 times a year.

28. Quarterly.

Describe a few of your friends of the library group's most effective fundraising events.

1. Book Store operated in a space within the library building. Annual Book Sale.

2. Casino was the most effective.

3. Library book sales.

4. Sale of donated books and magazines.

5. Library Lovers Calendar; Backstreet Books-used bookstore; Membership Drive; Jessie's Boutique (an annual women's gently used accessories sale); Jingle Books-Our end of year fundraiser for the next years book purchases- we kick this off on Give to the Max Day.

6. Bake sale, card sale, book shop.

7. Gala literary event.

8. Spring and Fall Book Sales, plus the 75th anniversary celebration for the library in the spring of 2012.

9. The most effective is c/o one group, which raises at least $14,000 per year with a Holiday Craft Bazaar, going strong for over thirty years. Another Friends group has pretty good success with seasonal bake sales.

10. Annual Christmas Homes Tour; Annual Basket Raffle at Cabin Fever Reliever.

11. Book and bake sales.

12. Book Sale; Christmas tree event.

13. Booksales ~ they have 4 per year.

14. We have a community wide garage sale twice a year. A large book sale once a year. They also accept private donations on the library's behalf.

15. Amazon online book sales and four book sales per year.

16. Christmas book basket silent auction; Book sale.

17. The Friends of the Library wrote a successful $25,000 joint grant with the

Lower Colorado River Authority to fund a water- conserving fountain for the Library's Courtyard. They have an in-library store, Buy the Book, and sell donated/weeded books online as well.

18. Library has an in-house bookstore that raises over $100 every month, we also host an annual vendor fair where the home-based party people buy a table for $25 then also donate part of the days proceeds back to the Library Friends. We have also done book-sales. We host an annual Wine and Dine event and a holiday decor sale where people donate their gently used and unwanted holiday decorations to the library. We set this up the week before Thanksgiving and it runs through Christmas week. Some items are special priced but 90% are just a free-will offering. We always make over $1000 on this event.

19. They recently hosted a "Founder's Day" type of event that raised $1,000.

20. The Friends of the Arlington Public Library raise funds to support the Library through their biannual book sales. They also have biannual Book and Author Luncheons, which raise awareness of the Friends and the Library, but they are not money-makers.

21. Sending books to Library Consignment and Better World Books.

22. Raffle of Technology products, Memorial Gifts, Book Sales.

23. Book Sale.

24. Bunko night, Spa day, silent auction, booksales.

25. A book sale, newspaper articles telling of things the library is raising money for, speaking to the senior center and the chamber of commerce.

26. Company donations and drives.

27. Chinese auction, annual book/street sale.

28. Wine and Beer Tasting with Silent Auction; Christmas Tree Sales (this was a past venture that is now done); Book Sales.

Chapter 3 – Book Sales and Sales of Other Intellectual Property

Table 9.1 How much did the library raise through book sales and the sales of other library materials such as DVDs, CDs, and magazines in 2012?

	Mean	Median	Minimum	Maximum
Entire sample	$6,674.75	$1,000.00	$0.00	$80,000.00

Table 9.2 How much did the library raise through book sales and the sales of other library materials such as DVDs, CDs, and magazines in 2012? Broken out by the existence of a "friends of the library" group.

Friends of Library Group	Mean	Median	Minimum	Maximum
Has a "friends of library" group	$9,122.87	$1,500.00	$0.00	$80,000.00
Does not have a "friends of library" group	$1,110.82	$322.00	$0.00	$7,566.00

Table 9.3 How much did the library raise through book sales and the sales of other library materials such as DVDs, CDs, and magazines in 2012? Broken out by total annual budget of the library, including spending for salaries and materials.

Budget	Mean	Median	Minimum	Maximum
Less than $100,000	$301.69	$70.00	$0.00	$1,900.00
$100,000 to $499,999	$2,288.42	$1,230.50	$0.00	$9,000.00
$500,000 or more	$18,991.62	$10,000.00	$0.00	$80,000.00

Table 9.4 How much did the library raise through book sales and the sales of other library materials such as DVDs, CDs, and magazines in 2012? Broken out by the size of the population served by the library.

Population Served	Mean	Median	Minimum	Maximum
Less than 2,500	$178.62	$30.00	$0.00	$500.00
2,500 to 19,999	$1,796.75	$1,480.50	$200.00	$7,100.00
20,000 or more	$19,673.44	$10,000.00	$0.00	$80,000.00

Table 9.5 How much did the library raise through book sales and the sales of other library materials such as DVDs, CDs, and magazines in 2012? Broken out by the amount of money raised from all sources through fundraising, grants, and donations in 2013.

Money Raised in 2013	Mean	Median	Minimum	Maximum
Less than $5,000	$4,924.77	$500.00	$0.00	$55,000.00
$5,000 to $14,999	$2,963.56	$500.00	$0.00	$14,402.00
$15,000 to $49,999	$6,155.00	$7,500.00	$30.00	$10,000.00
$50,000 or more	$14,083.36	$1,500.42	$0.00	$80,000.00

Table 10.1 How much did the library raise through book sales and the sales of other library materials such as DVDs, CDs, and magazines in 2013?

	Mean	Median	Minimum	Maximum
Entire sample	$6,659.78	$950.00	$0.00	$80,000.00

Table 10.2 How much did the library raise through book sales and the sales of other library materials such as DVDs, CDs, and magazines in 2013? Broken out by the existence of a "friends of the library" group.

Friends of Library Group	Mean	Median	Minimum	Maximum
Has a "friends of library" group	$9,189.00	$1,100.00	$0.00	$80,000.00
Does not have a "friends of library" group	$911.55	$100.00	$0.00	$5,700.00

Table 10.3 How much did the library raise through book sales and the sales of other library materials such as DVDs, CDs, and magazines in 2013? Broken out by total annual budget of the library, including spending for salaries and materials.

Budget	Mean	Median	Minimum	Maximum
Less than $100,000	$199.69	$45.00	$0.00	$1,050.00
$100,000 to $499,999	$2,240.08	$1,050.00	$0.00	$8,000.00
$500,000 or more	$19,115.90	$10,000.00	$0.00	$80,000.00

Table 10.4 How much did the library raise through book sales and the sales of other library materials such as DVDs, CDs, and magazines in 2013? Broken out by the size of the population served by the library.

Population Served	Mean	Median	Minimum	Maximum
Less than 2,500	$142.00	$15.00	$0.00	$500.00
2,500 to 19,999	$1,760.92	$1,075.00	$200.00	$7,500.00
20,000 or more	$19,706.81	$10,000.00	$0.00	$80,000.00

Table 10.5 How much did the library raise through book sales and the sales of other library materials such as DVDs, CDs, and magazines in 2013? Broken out by the amount of money raised from all sources through fundraising, grants, and donations in 2013.

Money Raised in 2013	Mean	Median	Minimum	Maximum
Less than $5,000	$5,225.85	$386.00	$0.00	$60,000.00
$5,000 to $14,999	$2,752.22	$500.00	$0.00	$14,010.00
$15,000 to $49,999	$6,075.00	$7,700.00	$0.00	$10,000.00
$50,000 or more	$13,824.49	$1,697.95	$0.00	$80,000.00

Table 11.1 Of the amount raised, approximately what percentage was from book sales?

	Mean	Median	Minimum	Maximum
Entire sample	84.25%	95.00%	0.00%	100.00%

Table 11.2 Of the amount raised, approximately what percentage was from book sales? Broken out by the existence of a "friends of the library" group.

Friends of Library Group	Mean	Median	Minimum	Maximum
Has a "friends of library" group	87.08%	92.50%	60.00%	100.00%
Does not have a "friends of library" group	76.14%	95.00%	0.00%	100.00%

Table 11.3 Of the amount raised, approximately what percentage was from book sales? Broken out by total annual budget of the library, including spending for salaries and materials.

Budget	Mean	Median	Minimum	Maximum
Less than $100,000	82.00%	100.00%	0.00%	100.00%
$100,000 to $499,999	86.10%	92.50%	60.00%	100.00%
$500,000 or more	84.46%	89.00%	66.00%	95.00%

Table 11.4 Of the amount raised, approximately what percentage was from book sales? Broken out by the size of the population served by the library.

Population Served	Mean	Median	Minimum	Maximum
Less than 2,500	81.44%	98.00%	0.00%	100.00%
2,500 to 19,999	87.27%	94.00%	65.00%	100.00%
20,000 or more	83.63%	89.00%	60.00%	95.00%

Table 11.5 Of the amount raised, approximately what percentage was from book sales? Broken out by the amount of money raised from all sources through fundraising, grants, and donations in 2013.

Money Raised in 2013	Mean	Median	Minimum	Maximum
Less than $5,000	85.85%	98.00%	55.00%	100.00%
$5,000 to $14,999	75.25%	86.50%	0.00%	100.00%
$15,000 to $49,999	90.00%	95.00%	65.00%	100.00%
$50,000 or more	90.00%	95.00%	80.00%	95.00%

Table 12.1 Of the amount raised, approximately what percentage was from periodicals?

	Mean	Median	Minimum	Maximum
Entire sample	4.83%	0.00%	0.00%	100.00%

Table 12.2 Of the amount raised, approximately what percentage was from periodicals? Broken out by the existence of a "friends of the library" group.

Friends of Library Group	Mean	Median	Minimum	Maximum
Has a "friends of library" group	1.14%	0.00%	0.00%	6.67%
Does not have a "friends of library" group	14.86%	0.00%	0.00%	100.00%

Table 12.3 Of the amount raised, approximately what percentage was from periodicals? Broken out by total annual budget of the library, including spending for salaries and materials.

Budget	Mean	Median	Minimum	Maximum
Less than $100,000	11.22%	0.00%	0.00%	100.00%
$100,000 to $499,999	0.89%	0.00%	0.00%	5.00%
$500,000 or more	2.08%	1.00%	0.00%	6.67%

Table 12.4 Of the amount raised, approximately what percentage was from periodicals? Broken out by the size of the population served by the library.

Population Served	Mean	Median	Minimum	Maximum
Less than 2,500	11.22%	0.00%	0.00%	100.00%
2,500 to 19,999	1.63%	0.00%	0.00%	6.67%
20,000 or more	1.25%	1.00%	0.00%	4.00%

Table 12.5 Of the amount raised, approximately what percentage was from periodicals? Broken out by the amount of money raised from all sources through fundraising, grants, and donations in 2013.

Money Raised in 2013	Mean	Median	Minimum	Maximum
Less than $5,000	1.08%	0.00%	0.00%	6.67%
$5,000 to $14,999	13.75%	0.50%	0.00%	100.00%
$15,000 to $49,999	0.40%	0.00%	0.00%	2.00%
$50,000 or more	1.00%	1.00%	0.00%	3.00%

Table 13.1 Of the amount raised, approximately what percentage was from sales of DVDs, CDs, and other non-print materials?

	Mean	Median	Minimum	Maximum
Entire sample	10.10%	4.00%	0.00%	45.00%

Table 13.2 Of the amount raised, approximately what percentage was from sales of DVDs, CDs, and other non-print materials? Broken out by the existence of a "friends of the library" group.

Friends of Library Group	Mean	Median	Minimum	Maximum
Has a "friends of library" group	10.48%	5.50%	0.00%	40.00%
Does not have a "friends of library" group	9.00%	1.00%	0.00%	45.00%

Table 13.3 Of the amount raised, approximately what percentage was from sales of DVDs, CDs, and other non-print materials? Broken out by total annual budget of the library, including spending for salaries and materials.

Budget	Mean	Median	Minimum	Maximum
Less than $100,000	6.78%	0.00%	0.00%	45.00%
$100,000 to $499,999	10.40%	5.50%	0.00%	40.00%
$500,000 or more	13.46%	9.00%	2.00%	33.00%

Table 13.4 Of the amount raised, approximately what percentage was from sales of DVDs, CDs, and other non-print materials? Broken out by the size of the population served by the library.

Population Served	Mean	Median	Minimum	Maximum
Less than 2,500	7.33%	0.00%	0.00%	45.00%
2,500 to 19,999	8.57%	4.00%	0.00%	26.67%
20,000 or more	15.13%	9.00%	2.00%	40.00%

Table 13.5 Of the amount raised, approximately what percentage was from sales of DVDs, CDs, and other non-print materials? Broken out by the amount of money raised from all sources through fundraising, grants, and donations in 2013.

Money Raised in 2013	Mean	Median	Minimum	Maximum
Less than $5,000	13.19%	2.00%	0.00%	45.00%
$5,000 to $14,999	11.00%	4.50%	0.00%	40.00%
$15,000 to $49,999	4.20%	5.00%	0.00%	10.00%
$50,000 or more	9.00%	4.00%	2.00%	20.00%

Table 14.1 Does the library have a book "wish list" that library patrons or browsers of the library website can view and then buy the book for the library from Amazon or some other bookseller?

	No Answer	Yes	No
Entire sample	2.44%	14.63%	82.93%

Table 14.2 Does the library have a book "wish list" that library patrons or browsers of the library website can view and then buy the book for the library from Amazon or some other bookseller? Broken out by the existence of a "friends of the library" group.

Friends of Library Group	No Answer	Yes	No
Has a "friends of library" group	3.33%	13.33%	83.33%
Does not have a "friends of library" group	0.00%	18.18%	81.82%

Table 14.3 Does the library have a book "wish list" that library patrons or browsers of the library website can view and then buy the book for the library from Amazon or some other bookseller? Broken out by total annual budget of the library, including spending for salaries and materials.

Budget	No Answer	Yes	No
Less than $100,000	0.00%	15.38%	84.62%
$100,000 to $499,999	0.00%	7.14%	92.86%
$500,000 or more	7.14%	21.43%	71.43%

Table 14.4 Does the library have a book "wish list" that library patrons or browsers of the library website can view and then buy the book for the library from Amazon or some other bookseller? Broken out by the size of the population served by the library.

Population Served	No Answer	Yes	No
Less than 2,500	0.00%	14.29%	85.71%
2,500 to 19,999	0.00%	7.69%	92.31%
20,000 or more	7.14%	21.43%	71.43%

Table 14.5 Does the library have a book "wish list" that library patrons or browsers of the library website can view and then buy the book for the library from Amazon or some other bookseller? Broken out by the amount of money raised from all sources through fundraising, grants, and donations in 2013.

Money Raised in 2013	No Answer	Yes	No
Less than $5,000	0.00%	15.38%	84.62%
$5,000 to $14,999	0.00%	10.00%	90.00%
$15,000 to $49,999	0.00%	14.29%	85.71%
$50,000 or more	9.09%	18.18%	72.73%

Table 15.1 If your library has such a wish list, how many books were purchased for the library through this system in the past year?

	Mean	Median	Minimum	Maximum
Entire sample	3,022.17	31.50	0.00	18,000.00

Table 15.2 If your library has such a wish list, how many books were purchased for the library through this system in the past year? Broken out by the existence of a "friends of the library" group.

Friends of Library Group	Mean	Median	Minimum	Maximum
Has a "friends of library" group	4,501.75	3.50	0.00	18,000.00
Does not have a "friends of library" group	63.00	63.00	58.00	68.00

Table 15.3 If your library has such a wish list, how many books were purchased for the library through this system in the past year? Broken out by total annual budget of the library, including spending for salaries and materials.

Budget	Mean	Median	Minimum	Maximum
Less than $100,000	63.00	63.00	58.00	68.00
$100,000 to $499,999	0.00	0.00	0.00	0.00
$500,000 or more	6,002.33	5.00	2.00	18,000.00

Table 15.4 If your library has such a wish list, how many books were purchased for the library through this system in the past year? Broken out by the size of the population served by the library.

Population Served	Mean	Median	Minimum	Maximum
Less than 2,500	63.00	63.00	58.00	68.00
2,500 to 19,999	0.00	0.00	0.00	0.00
20,000 or more	6,002.33	5.00	2.00	18,000.00

Table 15.5 If your library has such a wish list, how many books were purchased for the library through this system in the past year? Broken out by the amount of money raised from all sources through fundraising, grants, and donations in 2013.

Money Raised in 2013	Mean	Median	Minimum	Maximum
Less than $5,000	63.00	63.00	58.00	68.00
$5,000 to $14,999	0.00	0.00	0.00	0.00
$15,000 to $49,999	5.00	5.00	5.00	5.00
$50,000 or more	9,001.00	9,001.00	2.00	18,000.00

Chapter 4 – Annual Fund Drive

Table 16.1 Does your library have an annual fund drive?

	No Answer	Yes	No
Entire sample	0.00%	9.76%	90.24%

Table 16.2 Does your library have an annual fund drive? Broken out by the existence of a "friends of the library" group.

Friends of Library Group	Yes	No
Has a "friends of library" group	10.00%	90.00%
Does not have a "friends of library" group	9.09%	90.91%

Table 16.3 Does your library have an annual fund drive? Broken out by total annual budget of the library, including spending for salaries and materials.

Budget	Yes	No
Less than $100,000	0.00%	100.00%
$100,000 to $499,999	7.14%	92.86%
$500,000 or more	21.43%	78.57%

Table 16.4 Does your library have an annual fund drive? Broken out by the size of the population served by the library.

Population Served	Yes	No
Less than 2,500	0.00%	100.00%
2,500 to 19,999	7.69%	92.31%
20,000 or more	21.43%	78.57%

Table 16.5 Does your library have an annual fund drive? Broken out by the amount of money raised from all sources through fundraising, grants, and donations in 2013.

Money Raised in 2013	Yes	No
Less than $5,000	0.00%	100.00%
$5,000 to $14,999	10.00%	90.00%
$15,000 to $49,999	14.29%	85.71%
$50,000 or more	18.18%	81.82%

Table 17.1 What is the budget for the annual fund drive for labor, promotion (such as direct mail), phone calls, events, entertainment, and any other costs?

	Mean	Median	Minimum	Maximum
Entire sample	$2,375.00	$2,375.00	$750.00	$4,000.00

Table 17.2 What is the budget for the annual fund drive for labor, promotion (such as direct mail), phone calls, events, entertainment, and any other costs? Broken out by the existence of a "friends of the library" group.

Friends of Library Group	Mean	Median	Minimum	Maximum
Has a "friends of library" group	$750.00	$750.00	$750.00	$750.00
Does not have a "friends of library" group	$4,000.00	$4,000.00	$4,000.00	$4,000.00

Table 17.3 What is the budget for the annual fund drive for labor, promotion (such as direct mail), phone calls, events, entertainment, and any other costs? Broken out by total annual budget of the library, including spending for salaries and materials.

Budget	Mean	Median	Minimum	Maximum
Less than $100,000	N/A	N/A	N/A	N/A
$100,000 to $499,999	N/A	N/A	N/A	N/A
$500,000 or more	$2,375.00	$2,375.00	$750.00	$4,000.00

Table 17.4 What is the budget for the annual fund drive for labor, promotion (such as direct mail), phone calls, events, entertainment, and any other costs? Broken out by the size of the population served by the library.

Population Served	Mean	Median	Minimum	Maximum
Less than 2,500	N/A	N/A	N/A	N/A
2,500 to 19,999	N/A	N/A	N/A	N/A
20,000 or more	$2,375.00	$2,375.00	$750.00	$4,000.00

Table 17.5 What is the budget for the annual fund drive for labor, promotion (such as direct mail), phone calls, events, entertainment, and any other costs? Broken out by the amount of money raised from all sources through fundraising, grants, and donations in 2013.

Money Raised in 2013	Mean	Median	Minimum	Maximum
Less than $5,000	N/A	N/A	N/A	N/A
$5,000 to $14,999	N/A	N/A	N/A	N/A
$15,000 to $49,999	N/A	N/A	N/A	N/A
$50,000 or more	$2,375.00	$2,375.00	$750.00	$4,000.00

Table 18.1 How much did the library raise through the annual fund drive in 2012?

	Mean	Median	Minimum	Maximum
Entire sample	$14,700.25	$7,867.50	$1,500.00	$41,566.00

Table 18.2 How much did the library raise through the annual fund drive in 2012? Broken out by the existence of a "friends of the library" group.

Friends of Library Group	Mean	Median	Minimum	Maximum
Has a "friends of library" group	$5,745.00	$3,735.00	$1,500.00	$12,000.00
Does not have a "friends of library" group	$41,566.00	$41,566.00	$41,566.00	$41,566.00

Table 18.3 How much did the library raise through the annual fund drive in 2012? Broken out by total annual budget of the library, including spending for salaries and materials.

Budget	Mean	Median	Minimum	Maximum
Less than $100,000	N/A	N/A	N/A	N/A
$100,000 to $499,999	$3,735.00	$3,735.00	$3,735.00	$3,735.00
$500,000 or more	$18,355.33	$12,000.00	$1,500.00	$41,566.00

Table 18.4 How much did the library raise through the annual fund drive in 2012? Broken out by the size of the population served by the library.

Population Served	Mean	Median	Minimum	Maximum
Less than 2,500	N/A	N/A	N/A	N/A
2,500 to 19,999	$3,735.00	$3,735.00	$3,735.00	$3,735.00
20,000 or more	$18,355.33	$12,000.00	$1,500.00	$41,566.00

Table 18.5 How much did the library raise through the annual fund drive in 2012? Broken out by the amount of money raised from all sources through fundraising, grants, and donations in 2013.

Money Raised in 2013	Mean	Median	Minimum	Maximum
Less than $5,000	N/A	N/A	N/A	N/A
$5,000 to $14,999	$1,500.00	$1,500.00	$1,500.00	$1,500.00
$15,000 to $49,999	$3,735.00	$3,735.00	$3,735.00	$3,735.00
$50,000 or more	$26,783.00	$26,783.00	$12,000.00	$41,566.00

Table 19.1 How much did the library raise through the annual fund drive in 2013?

	Mean	Median	Minimum	Maximum
Entire sample	$5,323.33	$3,970.00	$0.00	$12,000.00

Table 19.2 How much did the library raise through the annual fund drive in 2013? Broken out by the existence of a "friends of the library" group.

Friends of Library Group	Mean	Median	Minimum	Maximum
Has a "friends of library" group	$5,323.33	$3,970.00	$0.00	$12,000.00
Does not have a "friends of library" group	N/A	N/A	N/A	N/A

Table 19.3 How much did the library raise through the annual fund drive in 2013? Broken out by total annual budget of the library, including spending for salaries and materials.

Budget	Mean	Median	Minimum	Maximum
Less than $100,000	N/A	N/A	N/A	N/A
$100,000 to $499,999	$3,970.00	$3,970.00	$3,970.00	$3,970.00
$500,000 or more	$6,000.00	$6,000.00	$0.00	$12,000.00

Table 19.4 How much did the library raise through the annual fund drive in 2013? Broken out by the size of the population served by the library.

Population Served	Mean	Median	Minimum	Maximum
Less than 2,500	N/A	N/A	N/A	N/A
2,500 to 19,999	$3,970.00	$3,970.00	$3,970.00	$3,970.00
20,000 or more	$6,000.00	$6,000.00	$0.00	$12,000.00

Table 19.5 How much did the library raise through the annual fund drive in 2013? Broken out by the amount of money raised from all sources through fundraising, grants, and donations in 2013.

Money Raised in 2013	Mean	Median	Minimum	Maximum
Less than $5,000	N/A	N/A	N/A	N/A
$5,000 to $14,999	$0.00	$0.00	$0.00	$0.00
$15,000 to $49,999	$3,970.00	$3,970.00	$3,970.00	$3,970.00
$50,000 or more	$12,000.00	$12,000.00	$12,000.00	$12,000.00

How has the library's annual fund strategy changed over the past five years? Is it relying more or less on direct mail? Have events come to play a more major role or not? Have costs increased or not? Comment on recent changes.

1. We do not raise money through events. Direct mail is our only means of fundraising.

2. We are trying to make the public more aware by newspaper articles, word of mouth, letting people know we have up-to-date technology, e-books which are new in the last year and a grant for children's books that some money had to be raised for and speaking to chamber and senior groups.

3. We don't have an annual fundraising strategy—unfortunately.

4. We have just initiated the direct mail for this fiscal year. We hope to increase attendance more than funding.

5. The Arlington Public Library Foundation has an annual campaign, but not the Library system. It is a direct mail campaign that typically brings in approximately $12,000.

6. We do not have one.

7. Very little.

8. Less direct mail. More social media and Constant Contact and email. More major events. Costs about the same-less on stamps -more on advertising.

9. Not really changed. They fall back on direct mail.

10. No annual fund drive, direct-mail newsletters to patrons and others that provide event info. Costs increase with postage and printing.

11. We use word of mouth about our non-profit status and people can give as they wish.

12. It has not changed. Advertising is done through our local newspaper, library fliers, and radio PSAs.

13. Library staff does not do fundraising except for specific grants that would apply to something we're doing. Same strategy for years

What is the single idea that most improved your results for your annual fund drive?

1. Personalized each letter by various Library Foundation Members.

2. Word of mouth! Success of Friends! Created a new area in our library for bookstore and coffee bar-a wifi internet cafe-has increased our exposure as the "place to connect" within our community.

3. Patrons want the children to have books so they were very supportive of raising $350 so we can get over $1,000 worth of books.

4. Targeting our mailings to those who have given for Capital Campaign or other in the past.

5. Radio PSAs.

Chapter 5 – Memorials, Tributes, and Trusts

Table 20.1 How much has the library cumulatively received through naming rights over the past three years?

	Mean	Median	Minimum	Maximum
Entire sample	$14,406.67	$0.00	$0.00	$500,000.00

Table 20.2 How much has the library cumulatively received through naming rights over the past three years? Broken out by the existence of a "friends of the library" group.

Friends of Library Group	Mean	Median	Minimum	Maximum
Has a "friends of library" group	$17,586.21	$0.00	$0.00	$500,000.00
Does not have a "friends of library" group	$5,186.00	$0.00	$0.00	$50,000.00

Table 20.3 How much has the library cumulatively received through naming rights over the past three years? Broken out by total annual budget of the library, including spending for salaries and materials.

Budget	Mean	Median	Minimum	Maximum
Less than $100,000	$833.33	$0.00	$0.00	$10,000.00
$100,000 to $499,999	$132.86	$0.00	$0.00	$1,860.00
$500,000 or more	$42,307.69	$0.00	$0.00	$500,000.00

Table 20.4 How much has the library cumulatively received through naming rights over the past three years? Broken out by the size of the population served by the library.

Population Served	Mean	Median	Minimum	Maximum
Less than 2,500	$0.00	$0.00	$0.00	$0.00
2,500 to 19,999	$912.31	$0.00	$0.00	$10,000.00
20,000 or more	$42,307.69	$0.00	$0.00	$500,000.00

Table 20.5 How much has the library cumulatively received through naming rights over the past three years? Broken out by the amount of money raised from all sources through fundraising, grants, and donations in 2013.

Money Raised in 2013	Mean	Median	Minimum	Maximum
Less than $5,000	$0.00	$0.00	$0.00	$0.00
$5,000 to $14,999	$1,111.11	$0.00	$0.00	$10,000.00
$15,000 to $49,999	$71,428.57	$0.00	$0.00	$500,000.00
$50,000 or more	$5,186.00	$0.00	$0.00	$50,000.00

Table 21.1 How much has the library cumulatively received through memorials over the past three years?

	Mean	Median	Minimum	Maximum
Entire sample	$4,507.28	$800.00	$0.00	$60,000.00

Table 21.2 How much has the library cumulatively received through memorials over the past three years? Broken out by the existence of a "friends of the library" group.

Friends of Library Group	Mean	Median	Minimum	Maximum
Has a "friends of library" group	$3,398.76	$800.00	$0.00	$25,400.00
Does not have a "friends of library" group	$7,722.00	$1,030.00	$0.00	$60,000.00

Table 21.3 How much has the library cumulatively received through memorials over the past three years? Broken out by total annual budget of the library, including spending for salaries and materials.

Budget	Mean	Median	Minimum	Maximum
Less than $100,000	$6,543.33	$1,220.00	$0.00	$60,000.00
$100,000 to $499,999	$2,771.43	$400.00	$0.00	$25,400.00
$500,000 or more	$4,497.23	$2,000.00	$0.00	$20,000.00

Table 21.4 How much has the library cumulatively received through memorials over the past three years? Broken out by the size of the population served by the library.

Population Served	Mean	Median	Minimum	Maximum
Less than 2,500	$5,829.23	$620.00	$0.00	$60,000.00
2,500 to 19,999	$3,180.00	$500.00	$0.00	$25,400.00
20,000 or more	$4,512.62	$2,000.00	$0.00	$20,000.00

Table 21.5 How much has the library cumulatively received through memorials over the past three years? Broken out by the amount of money raised from all sources through fundraising, grants, and donations in 2013.

Money Raised in 2013	Mean	Median	Minimum	Maximum
Less than $5,000	$1,564.62	$500.00	$0.00	$10,000.00
$5,000 to $14,999	$1,804.44	$1,440.00	$0.00	$5,000.00
$15,000 to $49,999	$5,805.71	$2,340.00	$0.00	$25,400.00
$50,000 or more	$9,856.40	$1,782.00	$0.00	$60,000.00

Table 22.1 How much has the library cumulatively received through tributes over the past three years?

	Mean	Median	Minimum	Maximum
Entire sample	$333.41	$0.00	$0.00	$5,000.00

Table 22.2 How much has the library cumulatively received through tributes over the past three years? Broken out by the existence of a "friends of the library" group.

Friends of Library Group	Mean	Median	Minimum	Maximum
Has a "friends of library" group	$206.90	$0.00	$0.00	$3,000.00
Does not have a "friends of library" group	$700.30	$0.00	$0.00	$5,000.00

Table 22.3 How much has the library cumulatively received through tributes over the past three years? Broken out by total annual budget of the library, including spending for salaries and materials.

Budget	Mean	Median	Minimum	Maximum
Less than $100,000	$166.92	$0.00	$0.00	$1,500.00
$100,000 to $499,999	$35.71	$0.00	$0.00	$300.00
$500,000 or more	$807.69	$0.00	$0.00	$5,000.00

Table 22.4 How much has the library cumulatively received through tributes over the past three years? Broken out by the size of the population served by the library.

Population Served	Mean	Median	Minimum	Maximum
Less than 2,500	$154.08	$0.00	$0.00	$1,500.00
2,500 to 19,999	$269.23	$0.00	$0.00	$3,000.00
20,000 or more	$576.92	$0.00	$0.00	$5,000.00

Table 22.5 How much has the library cumulatively received through tributes over the past three years? Broken out by the amount of money raised from all sources through fundraising, grants, and donations in 2013.

Money Raised in 2013	Mean	Median	Minimum	Maximum
Less than $5,000	$400.23	$0.00	$0.00	$3,000.00
$5,000 to $14,999	$111.11	$0.00	$0.00	$1,000.00
$15,000 to $49,999	$71.43	$0.00	$0.00	$500.00
$50,000 or more	$630.00	$0.00	$0.00	$5,000.00

Table 23.1 Has any sum of money or other tangible assets been left to the library in a will or through a trust in the past five years?

	No Answer	Yes	No
Entire sample	2.44%	46.34%	51.22%

Table 23.2 Has any sum of money or other tangible assets been left to the library in a will or through a trust in the past five years? Broken out by the existence of a "friends of the library" group.

Friends of Library Group	No Answer	Yes	No
Has a "friends of library" group	0.00%	46.67%	53.33%
Does not have a "friends of library" group	9.09%	45.45%	45.45%

Table 23.3 Has any sum of money or other tangible assets been left to the library in a will or through a trust in the past five years? Broken out by total annual budget of the library, including spending for salaries and materials.

Budget	No Answer	Yes	No
Less than $100,000	7.69%	38.46%	53.85%
$100,000 to $499,999	0.00%	50.00%	50.00%
$500,000 or more	0.00%	50.00%	50.00%

Table 23.4 Has any sum of money or other tangible assets been left to the library in a will or through a trust in the past five years? Broken out by the size of the population served by the library.

Population Served	No Answer	Yes	No
Less than 2,500	7.14%	28.57%	64.29%
2,500 to 19,999	0.00%	53.85%	46.15%
20,000 or more	0.00%	57.14%	42.86%

Table 23.5 Has any sum of money or other tangible assets been left to the library in a will or through a trust in the past five years? Broken out by the amount of money raised from all sources through fundraising, grants, and donations in 2013.

Money Raised in 2013	No Answer	Yes	No
Less than $5,000	7.69%	46.15%	46.15%
$5,000 to $14,999	0.00%	40.00%	60.00%
$15,000 to $49,999	0.00%	28.57%	71.43%
$50,000 or more	0.00%	63.64%	36.36%

Table 24.1 What is the monetary value of the total of what has been left to the library in wills or other bequests over the past five years?

	Mean	Median	Minimum	Maximum
Entire sample	$94,908.14	$35,000.00	$500.00	$775,000.00

Table 24.2 What is the monetary value of the total of what has been left to the library in wills or other bequests over the past five years? Broken out by the existence of a "friends of the library" group.

Friends of Library Group	Mean	Median	Minimum	Maximum
Has a "friends of library" group	$93,957.97	$25,000.00	$500.00	$775,000.00
Does not have a "friends of library" group	$97,378.60	$50,000.00	$1,500.00	$365,393.00

Table 24.3 What is the monetary value of the total of what has been left to the library in wills or other bequests over the past five years? Broken out by total annual budget of the library, including spending for salaries and materials.

Budget	Mean	Median	Minimum	Maximum
Less than $100,000	$22,600.00	$1,500.00	$500.00	$60,000.00
$100,000 to $499,999	$146,000.00	$45,000.00	$2,000.00	$775,000.00
$500,000 or more	$95,557.76	$43,976.79	$10,000.00	$365,393.00

Table 24.4 What is the monetary value of the total of what has been left to the library in wills or other bequests over the past five years? Broken out by the size of the population served by the library.

Population Served	Mean	Median	Minimum	Maximum
Less than 2,500	$15,750.00	$1,250.00	$500.00	$60,000.00
2,500 to 19,999	$151,000.00	$50,000.00	$2,000.00	$775,000.00
20,000 or more	$84,049.51	$25,000.00	$10,000.00	$365,393.00

Table 24.5 What is the monetary value of the total of what has been left to the library in wills or other bequests over the past five years? Broken out by the amount of money raised from all sources through fundraising, grants, and donations in 2013.

Money Raised in 2013	Mean	Median	Minimum	Maximum
Less than $5,000	$34,166.67	$1,750.00	$500.00	$100,000.00
$5,000 to $14,999	$40,000.00	$35,000.00	$15,000.00	$75,000.00
$15,000 to $49,999	$412,500.00	$412,500.00	$50,000.00	$775,000.00
$50,000 or more	$86,391.10	$35,000.00	$10,000.00	$365,393.00

Chapter 6 – Online Fundraising

Table 25.1 Does your library have a "donate" button (or similar function) on the library's website?

	No Answer	Yes	No
Entire sample	0.00%	14.63%	85.37%

Table 25.2 Does your library have a "donate" button (or similar function) on the library's website? Broken out by the existence of a "friends of the library" group.

Friends of Library Group	Yes	No
Has a "friends of library" group	20.00%	80.00%
Does not have a "friends of library" group	0.00%	100.00%

Table 25.3 Does your library have a "donate" button (or similar function) on the library's website? Broken out by total annual budget of the library, including spending for salaries and materials.

Budget	Yes	No
Less than $100,000	0.00%	100.00%
$100,000 to $499,999	7.14%	92.86%
$500,000 or more	35.71%	64.29%

Table 25.4 Does your library have a "donate" button (or similar function) on the library's website? Broken out by the size of the population served by the library.

Population Served	Yes	No
Less than 2,500	0.00%	100.00%
2,500 to 19,999	7.69%	92.31%
20,000 or more	35.71%	64.29%

Table 25.5 Does your library have a "donate" button (or similar function) on the library's website? Broken out by the amount of money raised from all sources through fundraising, grants, and donations in 2013.

Money Raised in 2013	Yes	No
Less than $5,000	0.00%	100.00%
$5,000 to $14,999	0.00%	100.00%
$15,000 to $49,999	42.86%	57.14%
$50,000 or more	27.27%	72.73%

Table 26.1 Does your library have a "donate" button (or similar function) on the library's Facebook page?

	No Answer	Yes	No
Entire sample	0.00%	0.00%	100.00%

Table 27.1 Does your library have a "donate" button (or similar function) on the library's blog?

	No Answer	Yes	No
Entire sample	0.00%	0.00%	100.00%

Table 28.1 Does your library have a "donate" button (or similar function) on the library's YouTube channel?

	No Answer	Yes	No
Entire sample	0.00%	0.00%	100.00%

Does your library have a "donate" button (or similar function) on any other venue?

1. Friends of the Library website.

2. Through the Library Foundation webpage.

3. On the Friends of the Library website.

Table 29.1 How much did the library raise specifically through online donations in 2012?

	Mean	Median	Minimum	Maximum
Entire sample	$808.56	$0.00	$0.00	$5,254.00

Table 29.2 How much did the library raise specifically through online donations in 2012? Broken out by the existence of a "friends of the library" group.

Friends of Library Group	Mean	Median	Minimum	Maximum
Has a "friends of library" group	$1,119.54	$0.00	$0.00	$5,254.00
Does not have a "friends of library" group	$0.00	$0.00	$0.00	$0.00

Table 29.3 How much did the library raise specifically through online donations in 2012? Broken out by total annual budget of the library, including spending for salaries and materials.

Budget	Mean	Median	Minimum	Maximum
Less than $100,000	$0.00	$0.00	$0.00	$0.00
$100,000 to $499,999	$950.00	$400.00	$0.00	$3,000.00
$500,000 or more	$1,792.33	$250.00	$0.00	$5,254.00

Table 29.4 How much did the library raise specifically through online donations in 2012? Broken out by the size of the population served by the library.

Population Served	Mean	Median	Minimum	Maximum
Less than 2,500	$0.00	$0.00	$0.00	$0.00
2,500 to 19,999	$633.33	$0.00	$0.00	$3,000.00
20,000 or more	$1,792.33	$250.00	$0.00	$5,254.00

Table 29.5 How much did the library raise specifically through online donations in 2012? Broken out by the amount of money raised from all sources through fundraising, grants, and donations in 2013.

Money Raised in 2013	Mean	Median	Minimum	Maximum
Less than $5,000	428.57	0.00	0.00	3000.00
$5,000 to $14,999	0.00	0.00	0.00	0.00
$15,000 to $49,999	266.67	0.00	0.00	800.00
$50,000 or more	2150.80	500.00	0.00	5254.00

Table 30.1 How much did the library raise specifically through online donations in 2013?

	Mean	Median	Minimum	Maximum
Entire sample	$994.44	$0.00	$0.00	$8,000.00

Table 30.2 How much did the library raise specifically through online donations in 2013? Broken out by the existence of a "friends of the library" group.

Friends of Library Group	Mean	Median	Minimum	Maximum
Has a "friends of library" group	$1,376.92	$0.00	$0.00	$8,000.00
Does not have a "friends of library" group	$0.00	$0.00	$0.00	$0.00

Table 30.3 How much did the library raise specifically through online donations in 2013? Broken out by total annual budget of the library, including spending for salaries and materials.

Budget	Mean	Median	Minimum	Maximum
Less than $100,000	$0.00	$0.00	$0.00	$0.00
$100,000 to $499,999	$1,100.00	$800.00	$0.00	$2,800.00
$500,000 or more	$2,250.00	$250.00	$0.00	$8,000.00

Table 30.4 How much did the library raise specifically through online donations in 2013? Broken out by the size of the population served by the library.

Population Served	Mean	Median	Minimum	Maximum
Less than 2,500	$0.00	$0.00	$0.00	$0.00
2,500 to 19,999	$733.33	$0.00	$0.00	$2,800.00
20,000 or more	$2,250.00	$250.00	$0.00	$8,000.00

Table 30.5 How much did the library raise specifically through online donations in 2013? Broken out by the amount of money raised from all sources through fundraising, grants, and donations in 2013.

Money Raised in 2013	Mean	Median	Minimum	Maximum
Less than $5,000	$400.00	$0.00	$0.00	$2,800.00
$5,000 to $14,999	$0.00	$0.00	$0.00	$0.00
$15,000 to $49,999	$533.33	$0.00	$0.00	$1,600.00
$50,000 or more	$2,700.00	$500.00	$0.00	$8,000.00

What has been your library's most effective means of online fundraising and how did you use it?

1. The Library Foundation also uses the online payments for the author event, a spring fundraising event.

2. The Arlington Public Library Foundation uses Sage Fundraising Online. One of the most effective uses is for registration for the Book It for Literacy 5K.

3. Through the Omaha Gives Event on May 22, 2013, via Omaha Community Foundation.

4. Give to the Max Day Jingle Books campaign sponsored by the JFHML Friends Foundation.

Chapter 7 – Development or Fundraising Staff

Table 31.1 Does the library have a fundraising or development staff?

	No Answer	Yes	No
Entire sample	0.00%	9.76%	90.24%

Table 31.2 Does the library have a fundraising or development staff? Broken out by the existence of a "friends of the library" group.

Friends of Library Group	Yes	No
Has a "friends of library" group	13.33%	86.67%
Does not have a "friends of library" group	0.00%	100.00%

Table 31.3 Does the library have a fundraising or development staff? Broken out by total annual budget of the library, including spending for salaries and materials.

Budget	Yes	No
Less than $100,000	7.69%	92.31%
$100,000 to $499,999	0.00%	100.00%
$500,000 or more	21.43%	78.57%

Table 31.4 Does the library have a fundraising or development staff? Broken out by the size of the population served by the library.

Population Served	Yes	No
Less than 2,500	7.14%	92.86%
2,500 to 19,999	0.00%	100.00%
20,000 or more	21.43%	78.57%

Table 31.5 Does the library have a fundraising or development staff? Broken out by the amount of money raised from all sources through fundraising, grants, and donations in 2013.

Money Raised in 2013	Yes	No
Less than $5,000	7.69%	92.31%
$5,000 to $14,999	0.00%	100.00%
$15,000 to $49,999	0.00%	100.00%
$50,000 or more	27.27%	72.73%

What has been the budget trend for the library's development or fundraising staff over the past two years? Has its budget increased or decreased? If so, by how much? What is the outlook for the future?

1. Same budget. No changes in sight.

2. No budget except for salary.

3. Small increases from cities served.

4. The budget has been about the same for the last 3 years.

5. For now it has not increased but the board and community members are working to raise money for a handicap accessible library.

6. Fundraising brought in in FY13 decreased 9% from what was brought in in FY12. We are hopeful that amount will increase in FY14.

Please describe some of the most effective fundraising special events staged or held by the library, the friends of the library, a library foundation, or any other group.

1. Library Foundation author event usually yields around $6,000.

2. Gala literary event staged by foundation.

3. A luncheon at the local school auction. Movie Matinees. Summer Reading Program. Early Out Program.

4. Our Wine and Dine is an annual event that always raises about the same amount of money ($1,700) but the awareness for the library is very good and I believe it has led to other donations down the line.

5. Yearly fall event with silent auction, sponsorships and advertisement opportunities. Event transforms the library into different destinations then offers food, entertainment and decor from that destination.

6. An evening with Laura Bush raised over $10,000.

7. The library has held an adult spelling bee annually.

8. Book sales.

9. In 2012 we held a soup supper that brought in $443. In 2012 we served lunch after our summer Big Days event that brought in $876.54 (that event has been discontinued now). In 2013 we held a breakfast that brought in $191.31.

10. Foundations have been a good source with community matching a donation. Silent Book basket auction.

11. Book It for Literacy 5K. Author events with well known authors (Sandra Brown, Nora Roberts).

12. None staged for this purpose. We participate each year in the Cotulla Country Christmas put on by the local Chamber of Commerce, where we have books for sale and where we also have a Christmas StoryTime each hour to demonstrate one of our services.

13. We have a booth at our annual 4th of July event. The teens work this event and sell concessions, glow toys and other things to raise money.

14. Bake sales.

15. Our anniversary event, already mentioned, raised about $7,500; our 50th event for the branch library raised about $5,000; and an "Antiques Roadshow" program raised about $2,000.

16. Besides those mentioned earlier gumball sales are surprisingly good. Photos with Santa are also good.

17. Again, one Friends group is very successful with its annual Holiday Bazaar--a craft fair a week or so before Thanksgiving.

18. Book sales.

19. Annual book/street sale and Chinese auction.

20. Wine and Beer Tasting with Silent Auction.

21. Library Foundation holds an annual Library MiniGolf event ~ 18 holes of minigolf inside the library. The Friends of the Library have quarterly book sales which are very well attended and always successful.

22. We have held food stand for a local band concert and host a vendor fundraiser where people can come and shop for gifts and 10% of the profits goes to the library.

23. Speaking to the chamber of commerce and this information is published in our local newspaper. Information is sent around businesses in town, and the book sale goes to pay for our e-book renewal each year. The library foundation and community members are in the process of raising funds for a handicap accessible library.

24. Annual Book and Author Luncheon. Annual Book Sale.

Chapter 8 – Grants

Table 32.1 How much did the library raise through grants in 2012?

	Mean	Median	Minimum	Maximum
Entire sample	$27,500.03	$1,125.00	$0.00	$438,261.00

Table 32.2 How much did the library raise through grants in 2012? Broken out by the existence of a "friends of the library" group.

Friends of Library Group	Mean	Median	Minimum	Maximum
Has a "friends of library" group	$37,592.29	$3,850.00	$0.00	$438,261.00
Does not have a "friends of library" group	$3,278.60	$550.00	$0.00	$19,736.00

Table 32.3 How much did the library raise through grants in 2012? Broken out by total annual budget of the library, including spending for salaries and materials.

Budget	Mean	Median	Minimum	Maximum
Less than $100,000	$2,212.50	$250.00	$0.00	$15,000.00
$100,000 to $499,999	$8,769.00	$3,850.00	$0.00	$38,000.00
$500,000 or more	$68,396.75	$7,500.00	$0.00	$438,261.00

Table 32.4 How much did the library raise through grants in 2012? Broken out by the size of the population served by the library.

Population Served	Mean	Median	Minimum	Maximum
Less than 2,500	$3,859.45	$600.00	$0.00	$15,904.00
2,500 to 19,999	$8,507.82	$1,500.00	$0.00	$38,000.00
20,000 or more	$66,580.08	$4,850.00	$0.00	$438,261.00

Table 32.5 How much did the library raise through grants in 2012? Broken out by the amount of money raised from all sources through fundraising, grants, and donations in 2013.

Money Raised in 2013	Mean	Median	Minimum	Maximum
Less than $5,000	$3,420.00	$725.00	$0.00	$15,000.00
$5,000 to $14,999	$1,271.43	$500.00	$0.00	$4,700.00
$15,000 to $49,999	$11,234.00	$6,750.00	$0.00	$38,000.00
$50,000 or more	$74,954.27	$10,000.00	$0.00	$438,261.00

Table 33.1 How much did the library raise through grants in 2013?

	Mean	Median	Minimum	Maximum
Entire sample	$27,774.69	$1,000.00	$0.00	$383,624.00

Table 33.2 How much did the library raise through grants in 2013? Broken out by the existence of a "friends of the library" group.

Friends of Library Group	Mean	Median	Minimum	Maximum
Has a "friends of library" group	$35,199.33	$3,000.00	$0.00	$383,624.00
Does not have a "friends of library" group	$11,575.45	$800.00	$0.00	$112,283.00

Table 33.3 How much did the library raise through grants in 2013? Broken out by total annual budget of the library, including spending for salaries and materials.

Budget	Mean	Median	Minimum	Maximum
Less than $100,000	$1,980.54	$700.00	$0.00	$10,000.00
$100,000 to $499,999	$20,224.30	$5,100.00	$0.00	$112,283.00
$500,000 or more	$62,010.33	$3,750.00	$0.00	$383,624.00

Table 33.4 How much did the library raise through grants in 2013? Broken out by the size of the population served by the library.

Population Served	Mean	Median	Minimum	Maximum
Less than 2,500	$3,800.58	$900.00	$0.00	$19,860.00
2,500 to 19,999	$17,107.55	$1,500.00	$0.00	$112,283.00
20,000 or more	$61,527.00	$3,350.00	$0.00	$383,624.00

Table 33.5 How much did the library raise through grants in 2013? Broken out by the amount of money raised from all sources through fundraising, grants, and donations in 2013.

Money Raised in 2013	Mean	Median	Minimum	Maximum
Less than $5,000	$1,714.70	$750.00	$0.00	$6,647.00
$5,000 to $14,999	$2,150.00	$950.00	$0.00	$5,700.00
$15,000 to $49,999	$11,643.33	$12,500.00	$0.00	$25,000.00
$50,000 or more	$78,900.64	$10,000.00	$0.00	$383,624.00

Table 34.1 How much manpower did the library expend in trying to obtain grants in the past year?*

	Mean	Median	Minimum	Maximum
Entire sample	202.07	50.00	0.00	1,560.00

Table 34.2 How much manpower did the library expend in trying to obtain grants in the past year? Broken out by the existence of a "friends of the library" group.

Friends of Library Group	Mean	Median	Minimum	Maximum
Has a "friends of library" group	241.80	40.00	0.00	1,560.00
Does not have a "friends of library" group	122.60	55.00	0.00	600.00

Table 34.3 How much manpower did the library expend in trying to obtain grants in the past year? Broken out by total annual budget of the library, including spending for salaries and materials.

Budget	Mean	Median	Minimum	Maximum
Less than $100,000	139.09	60.00	0.00	600.00
$100,000 to $499,999	148.38	43.00	0.00	600.00
$500,000 or more	304.09	40.00	0.00	1,560.00

* If one full-time employee spent all of his/her time on grant applications, this would be 1,800 hours.

Table 34.4 How much manpower did the library expend in trying to obtain grants in the past year? Broken out by the size of the population served by the library.

Population Served	Mean	Median	Minimum	Maximum
Less than 2,500	153.00	90.00	0.00	600.00
2,500 to 19,999	113.00	30.00	0.00	600.00
20,000 or more	319.55	40.00	0.00	1,560.00

Table 34.5 How much manpower did the library expend in trying to obtain grants in the past year? Broken out by the amount of money raised from all sources through fundraising, grants, and donations in 2013.

Money Raised in 2013	Mean	Median	Minimum	Maximum
Less than $5,000	119.29	25.00	0.00	600.00
$5,000 to $14,999	103.00	50.00	0.00	300.00
$15,000 to $49,999	108.00	40.00	0.00	300.00
$50,000 or more	360.55	50.00	0.00	1,560.00

Please name some of the library's most important grants received over the past five years and, if possible, the amount and source.

1. Texas Book Festival Grant, McKenna Foundation Grant.

2. Tiesons, Walmart.

3. Bremer Bank $36,750; Initiative Foundation $10,000; Hallett Trust $19,200.

4. New Horizon's Grant - Canadian Government $20,000.

5. Our biggest was close to $50,000 through LSTA for a Community Entrepreneurial Office (CEO). We were getting $30,000 a year through the county youth initiative, MyCom, for both a Homework Center and our Teen programs, but we are no longer getting the 50% for teens.

6. J. Frank Dobie Trust - 2013 $5,000 Ladd and Katherine Hancher Foundation - 2013 $8,360.

7. From local foundations for tuck pointing historical building and new roof. Dolly Parton Imagination Library, databases, art exhibits, programs.

8. Enhance Hamilton County Foundation.

9. Grant for $5,000 for special-category books - Tocker Foundation. Will be applying for grants in 2014 for grants to purchase books for branch to be opened in the county, and to purchase more computers.

10. BTOP grant for new computers, printers, desks, ADA computer form the Nebraska Library Commission and the Bill and Melinda Gates foundation. Grants from the LibriFoundation for over $1,000 which can be reapplied for every 3 years.

11. Matching CEDC/Friends grant - $3,000. Excel $1,000.

12. Michael and Susan Dell Foundation $187,000

13. Technology/filtering grant, State Library of Ohio, $1,500.

14. Paint Iowa Beautiful grant sponsored by Diamond Vogel. We received 8 gallons of paint of whatever type we chose.

15. CACHF grant for health resources LSTA grant to digitize resources Focus on energy grant to upgrade boiler.

16. Co Serv $10,000 for new patron computers.

17. Kreutz Bennett grant for library remodel $8,500. Rotary Club for new windows $10,000.

18. Hearst Foundation-$25,000 National Endowment of Arts-$13,000

19. Dollar General for literacy Arlington Tomorrow Foundation for various amounts and purposes Texas State Library and Archives Commission - several grants and purposes IMLS National Leadership grant for early childhood Arlington Independent School District for literacy.

20. Lone Star Library Grant, WalMart Grant.

21. Batterman Foundation.

22. Libri Foundation Grant, $2,000 in books.

23. Winnie Bell $400.00.

24. 2013: Libri matching foundation - we got $1160 worth of new children's books. Iowa Library Technology Grant for $987.66 to update our technology. Target grant for our after school programs $2000.

25. Eastern Iowa Grant Foundation

26. Just $600 c/o a Virginia Breast Cancer Foundation grant for related materials (books, DVDs).

27. Broadband Stimulus grant through our State Library System and the Gates Foundation...this gave our library over 35,000 in equipment and software in 2011/12.

28. LCRA, TexTreasures

29. Praxair Grant Katherine and Ladd Hancher Foundation

What are your favorite information sources about library fundraising? Mention blogs, listservs, conferences, and other sources that have been useful to you.

1. ALA Center of Philanthropy.

2. AFP meetings, American Libraries.

3. Email newsletters, library system memos.

4. I use libraryworks.com.

5. Basically, just forwarded emails c/o the Library of Virginia's Development and Networking Division.

6. State Library of Iowa, ALA, ILA.

7. State Library of Iowa listserv.

8. We do not have such sources.

9. Consultant Lori Jacobwith – Telling Your Library Story

10. Conferences, word of mouth, State Library.

11. Iowa Library listserv.

12. Listservs and blogs.

13. Our local system newsletter, online articles, ideas from our friends members.

14. Listservs.

15. PLANT listserv, State Library listserv, TLA emails, Amigos emails.

16. AFP Texas State Library.

17. Texas Library Association website.

18. State library of Iowa Dallas Cinty Foundation.

19. Grant Siren: grantalert@grantwriters.net.

20. No special source.

21. Conferences, ALA website for Friends/Foundations.

22. Newspaper articles, word of mouth, a group who is now putting together a package and going out to people of the community asking for donations for a new handicap accessible library hopefully by 2016.

www.ingramcontent.com/pod-product-compliance
Lightning Source LLC
Chambersburg PA
CBHW081355230426
43667CB00017B/2842